Innovate the Future

Innovate the Future

A Radical New Approach to IT Innovation

David Croslin

PRENTICE
HALL

Upper Saddle River, NJ • Boston • Indianapolis • San Francisco
New York • Toronto • Montreal • London • Munich • Paris • Madrid
Capetown • Sydney • Tokyo • Singapore • Mexico City

Many of the designations used by manufacturers and sellers to distinguish their products are claimed as trademarks. Where those designations appear in this book, and the publisher was aware of a trademark claim, the designations have been printed with initial capital letters or in all capitals.

The author and publisher have taken care in the preparation of this book, but make no expressed or implied warranty of any kind and assume no responsibility for errors or omissions. No liability is assumed for incidental or consequential damages in connection with or arising out of the use of the information or programs contained herein.

The publisher offers excellent discounts on this book when ordered in quantity for bulk purchases or special sales, which may include electronic versions and/or custom covers and content particular to your business, training goals, marketing focus, and branding interests. For more information, please contact:

> U.S. Corporate and Government Sales
> (800) 382-3419
> corpsales@pearsontechgroup.com

For sales outside the United States please contact:

> International Sales
> international@pearson.com

Visit us on the Web: informit.com/ph

Library of Congress Cataloging-in-Publication Data

Croslin, David.
   Innovate the future : a radical new approach to IT innovation / David Croslin.
        p. cm.
   Includes index.
   ISBN 978-0-13-705515-9 (pbk. : alk. paper)
   1. Technological innovations. 2. Information technology–Management. I. Title.
   T173.8.C765 2010
   658'.05–dc22

                                                  2010007206

ISBN-13: 978-0-13-705515-9
ISBN-10:   0-13-705515-3
Text printed in the United States on recycled paper at Courier in Stoughton, Massachusetts.
First printing, April 2010

Associate Publisher
Greg Wiegand

Sr. Acquisitions Editor
Katherine Bull

Development Editor
Julie Bess

Managing Editor
John Fuller

Project Editor
Anna Popick

Copy Editor
Kim Wimpsett

Indexer
Michael Loo

Proofreader
Linda Begley

Cover Designer
Alan Clements

Compositor
Rob Mauhar

This book is dedicated to the people who have made me stronger by supporting me when I was weak. It's dedicated to my loved and loving wife, Suzanne, and my amazing children—Jessica, Bonnie, Kaitlyn, Kristina, Olivia, Jolie, Parker, and Hunter—for the sacrifices you have made during the writing of this book. It's dedicated to my best friends and mentors for cheering me on when I was right but more so for guiding me when I was wrong. And it's dedicated to Bob Laird, whose friendship, mentorship, and guidance made this book possible.

Contents

Acknowledgments

I would like to thank Bob Laird, my brilliant best friend, for all of his support while I was writing this book. Bob planted the seed for *Innovate the Future* and kicked me hard enough to make me write it. Writing a book, I have now discovered, can be an agonizing experience filled with countless hours of exploration, frustration, and self-doubt. Bob was my constant guide, never accepting less from me than he knew I was capable of. The "shine" this book may deliver is due mostly to Bob's support.

I would also like to thank my mentors who listened to me drone on and on about different topics, issues, and challenges from the book and yet kept coming back for more. Writing a book, almost as much as borrowing money, can truly test the bonds of friendship. Thank you to Craig Young, the best project manager on the planet, who taught me to find the value in small details. Thanks to Allen Proithis, the best business development executive and networker anywhere, who taught me to attack in a million different directions at once and showed me the true value of networking. Thanks to Larry Commerford, one of the most brilliant technology people I have ever met, who shook his head at me a thousand times and taught me how broadly ideas can penetrate if you open your eyes and mind.

Many thanks go to Katherine Bull, my acquisitions editor at Pearson Education, who patiently guided me through the writing, delivery, and production of this book. Thanks go as well to the many editors and the production and marketing teams.

Thanks to the stalwart reviewers who added their two cents, and often a great deal more, of advice throughout the book: Brad Barbera, Roy Bynum, Bob Laird, Benjamin Solomon, and Jim Woods.

Finally, thanks to my ever-growing, global network of friends and associates who discussed a thousand different topics related to invention and innovation with me. It never ceases to amaze me how many wonderful and imaginative people there are in this amazing world of ours.

About the Author

David Croslin is the president of Innovate the Future, a consultancy special-izing in customer, product, and market innovation. Previously, David was the chief technologist at Hewlett-Packard in the $12 billion Communications, Media, and Entertainment division, and prior to that he was the chief prod-uct architect at Verizon Business and MCI. He has twenty-five granted patents and is a frequent speaker at global conferences including CTIA, TMForum, Billing and OSS World, and Mobile World Congress. He is a frequent advisor to technology firms, venture capital firms, and fund managers, and he works with numerous start-ups as a C-level executive and board member. David runs the LinkedIn group "Innovate the Future" with more than two-thousand distinguished innovators in seventy countries.

PART I
Understanding Innovation

1

Inventions and Innovations

Have you ever wondered why the company you are working for now or worked at in the past was willing to put money into research and development for one product while denying funding for another? Or have you wondered why some additional product features for an existing product were funded while another set was not? Did you think all of those decisions made sense or were arbitrary and capricious?

How many times have you had a great idea that you didn't follow up on, only to find a year later that a complete stranger not only had the same idea but turned it into an actual invention with a patent and a market? Did you kick yourself because that person has fame and fortune and you don't?

Not many of us have the genius of Thomas Edison, yet as Edison said, "Genius is 1% inspiration and 99% perspiration." Why is it that some ideas just stay ideas, other ideas become interesting inventions, while yet other ideas not only become inventions but are considered so innovative that they change how people lead their lives? Edison had the ideas and the work ethic to try to repeatedly fail. In spite of those failures, he ended up with 1,093 patents and created the lightbulb and electricity, the phonograph, and film projectors and motion pictures.

So, what's the difference between an idea, an invention, and an innovation? Is the process truly random and subject to finding an Edison, or is there a process to help the transition along? What are the different types of inventions from the point of view of business versus technical and internal versus external? What are the different types of innovation, and how should we think about and consider them?

It's important as a foundation for understanding the rest of the book that we understand these questions and start to garner some idea about the difference between ideas, different types of inventions, and different types of innovations.

3

Inventions and Innovations

Two of the most important and distinctive utilizations of the words *invention* and *innovation* demonstrate how far apart people's perceptions can be. The following are two utilizations, critical to defining the extreme ends of the invention/innovation process:

- Patents are granted for inventions, not innovations.

- Customers buy innovative products, not inventive products.

It is important that the business processes used to identify and deploy innovations take into account that there is a tremendous difference between coming up with an idea, turning the idea into an invention, and finally evolving the invention into an innovation. Figure 1.1 shows these three ever-higher, more difficult to achieve planes of idea, invention, and innovation. It is critical to understand the transformative impact and value of the idea and the invention on a consumer's lifestyle.

An invention is something that is created from an idea. For example, an invention could be a new manufacturing method, a new product feature, or a new internal business process. It is important to realize that the mere definition of an invention does not make it intrinsically valuable. It often has a potential value and is therefore categorized as intellectual property. But, until it is deployed in some way, it should not be considered an innovation.

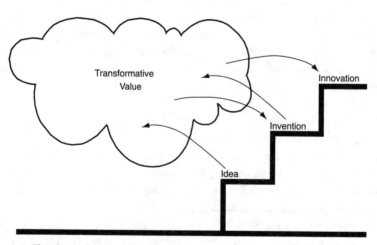

FIGURE 1.1   The three planes of idea, invention, and innovation

Once an invention is implemented, packaged, marketed, and deployed, it still may not be an innovation. At this point, it is only a new product, method, or feature. If the product is poorly marketed or poorly accepted, then the invention may not have the potential to become a true innovation. Or, the limitation may be in the packaging, marketing, or price, and the invention still retains innovation potential.

Only after a deployed invention has been used and accepted by the consumer and has been deemed by the consumer to add some form of real, positive, and transformative value will the consumer perceive the original invention as an "innovative" product. It is at this point when the consumer perceives some degree of transformative value that the original invention and the deployed product that utilizes the invention both become branded as an innovation and the common blending of the words *invention* and *innovation* occurs.

As illustrated in Figure 1.2, many terms apply throughout an invention-to-innovation process. Inventions start out as discoveries that create a new technology, define a new approach, and fulfill a perceived need. If a discovery is then deemed to have possible value, the discoverers will utilize the invention by creating a product or a process resulting in intellectual property, patents, and assets.

Once an invention has been "fleshed out" into a utilizable product, it can then be marketed. It is through the marketing process that the original discovery is introduced to the consumer. How the consumer perceives and utilizes the product and then how the consumer subsequently values the deployed product determines whether the product is merely competitive with

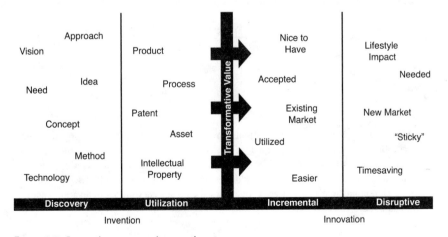

FIGURE 1.2 Inventions versus innovations

existing products or is innovative to some degree. This could be summarized as a product's **transformative value** or **transformative impact**. In other words, how much does the new product transform a consumer's life or business?

New products that deliver no real transformative value are merely competitive and in a consumer's eyes have delivered no new properties that the consumer would perceive as innovative. The introduction of a flashy new cell phone model but with no new features should be considered as merely competitive in nature. Such innovations deliver only incremental value to an already existing market.

The introduction of a new product that creates a new market, that is described as "needed," and that has a real, identifiable transformative impact on consumer and business lifestyles would be described as a disruptive innovation. The introduction of the Apple iPhone and the RIM BlackBerry created the smartphone market. Although primarily still cell phones in nature, smartphones had features that created a lifestyle and timesaving impact that is transformative.

We will discuss how to force inventions to become innovations in later chapters.

BOB SHOULD CONSIDER[1]

- Have we identified what our customers would consider innovative?
- How do we define the transformative value of our products?
- Do we have the inventions needed for new innovations?
- Are we pursuing competitive, incremental, or disruptive innovations?

---

1. Throughout the book, we will use a "Bob Should Consider" section to specify the questions that a fictitious innovation expert named Bob would be asking as he ponders the aspects of innovation that we have just discussed in the book. These questions are meant both to summarize the main points of the prior discussion and to provide an initial set of specific discussion points that you and your colleagues should consider for the innovation opportunity at hand.

Inventions and Randomness

Many companies encourage their employees to be inventive and provide suggestions, no matter how big or small. They say things like "We need every employee to be inventive. No idea is a bad idea. All ideas will be considered for our new products." Although we are not saying this is a bad idea, such ideas will tend to be incremental and not transformative. Employees are expected to do more with less these days, and few have the time to think about anything outside their bailiwick. Simply, it's not how a transformative innovation process will typically take place.

If I were to blindfold you and ask you to find the single blue marble in a bucket of 100 red marbles, your chances for success would be very limited, especially if every time you pulled out the incorrect marble you had to return it to the bucket. The invention and innovation processes currently utilized by many companies do not vary a great deal from this seemingly endless and fruitless process. Ideas are proposed, quickly reviewed, and then either discarded or scheduled for further evaluation.

I describe this current invention and innovation process as being "random" in nature. The typical innovation process has quite an element of pure chance involved. The processes that companies implement, often based on input from innovation consultants, are designed to maximize the potential for finding viable inventions in spite of the underlying randomness of the process.

Generally, the current invention and innovation processes, such as they are, attempt to reduce the impacts of this randomness by proposing that companies follow three primary innovation rules, as listed here and depicted in Figure 1.3. These innovation rules are not significantly different from many approaches of increasing your chances of winning the lottery:

- **Increase the number of inventors:** This is done by "empowering" all the employees, creating innovation teams, and so on. Increasing the number of inventors, just like buying more lottery tickets, increases the probability that you might hit a winner.

- **Increase the odds of recognizing a potentially viable invention:** This is done by changing the way managers work with their teams, creating innovation review councils, and so on. When managers are taught how to calculate the odds of winning a particular lottery game, then they can maximize potential wins by ensuring employees play in the right games.

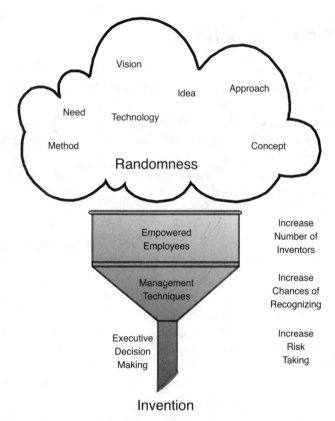

FIGURE 1.3 Inventions and randomness

- Increase the number of attempts the company tries to deploy new inventions: This involves greater risk and requires changing the decision-making and investing process of the executive team. Essentially, the thought here is that the more times a company plays in the innovation lottery, the more likely it is to win.

Google is almost universally regarded as a highly innovative company. Google follows the common innovation rules:

- Google allows its employees to spend 20% of their work week innovating relative to any topic they want.
- Google has monthly innovation review meetings and open-door policies to allow employees free access to management.

- Google executives are willing to deploy virtually any reasonable invention on a beta prototype basis and allow the employees to maintain it during their 20% innovation time.

Google's goals for implementing these internal innovation policies are twofold:

- Find ways to generate additional revenues from search advertising.

- Find new products, markets, and revenue streams that are not dependent on advertising.

Google has succeeded tremendously at the first goal of increasing ways to deliver ads and increasing search advertising revenues. The introduction of astounding new innovations such as Google Earth has succeeded in changing the very name *Google* from a noun into a verb, as in "to Google." Google has succeeded tremendously at deploying incremental innovations that maximize the benefit of its original disruptive innovation. We will discuss later in this chapter the concepts of incremental and disruptive innovation.

With regard to the second goal of becoming less dependent on a single revenue stream, Google has been much less successful. In Google's latest annual report, the company states, "Advertising revenues made up 99% of our revenues in 2006 and 2007 and 97% of our revenues in 2008. We derive most of our additional revenues from offering internet ad serving and management services to advertisers and ad agencies, the license of our web search technology and the license of our search solutions to enterprises."[2]

As we shall see later, the perceived randomness of the current invention process, and similarly the randomness of the innovation process, can be eliminated by following a targeted invention and innovation process.

BOB SHOULD CONSIDER

- Do our invention and innovation processes have an underlying foundation of randomness?

- If we are trying to be transformative, when we select ideas for generating new products, are we considering the transformative impact on our customers of those products?

- How much are our invention and innovation processes costing us because of the underlying randomness?

---

2. Google, Inc. Annual report, form 10-K. Filing date 2/13/2009, p. 38.

Types of Inventions

Not all inventions are created equally. They are particularly different in how those inventions can be evolved into marketable products. Having an understanding how companies create inventions, how those inventions should be properly treated as intellectual property, and how that intellectual property can be used to create new product innovations is critical. Inventions can be divided into three major categories, as depicted in Figure 1.4. These categories are defined as follows:

- **Foundational invention:** Foundational inventions create a basis for application. They are very much a new form of a "raw material." Examples could be the invention of nylon or the transistor. Although the invention is valuable by itself, the true transformative value lies in the applications of the foundational invention to create inventions in the other two categories of invention: functional and product.

- **Functional invention:** Functional inventions are generally an application of a foundational invention. Functional inventions can become a product innovation directly as in the case of Velcro (which makes use of nylon) or an integrated circuit (which makes use of transistors). The functional invention can also be used as a component of the third invention category: product invention.

- **Product invention:** Product inventions are the integration of one or more foundational, functional, and/or product inventions. For

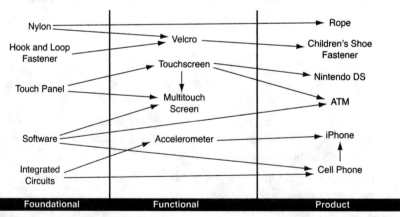

FIGURE 1.4 Types of inventions

instance, the use of Velcro on children's shoes or in other situations where knots might come undone is an example of a product invention that utilizes a functional invention (Velcro) that is based on a foundational invention (nylon).

Each of these types of inventions, once developed into a product, marketed, and accepted can become an innovation. Parents love Velcro shoe ties for their kids, but they rarely think, "Wow, nylon is so cool and innovative."

Depending on the type of business lifestyle (job) or personal lifestyle a consumer has and how specific invention types apply to those lifestyles, each of these three types of invention (foundational, functional, or product) can be viewed as equally innovative. The key for all of them, however, is still the degree of transformative impact and value.

BOB SHOULD CONSIDER

- What kind of inventions do we own?
- Are our inventions foundational, functional, or products?
- What kind of inventions do we want to create?
- What kinds of inventions are needed for us to create new, innovative products?

Business versus Technical Invention

Inventions are not limited to physical creations as the previous discussion might imply. Business inventions often take the form of a logical business process. These logical business processes can then be manifested physically by implementation within software packages or computer hardware or even can be mechanized through the use of physical implementations such as robots on an assembly line. When considering invention and innovation processes as well as determining the transformative value or impact of an invention, it is important to understand why particular inventions have the transformative impact that they do and what the underlying concepts of the invention are. With this in mind, inventions can also be classified by the types of creations they are based on:

- Conceptual inventions such as a political system like democracy
- Logical inventions such as project management techniques
- Physical inventions such as an electric motor or an Apple iPod

Conceptual inventions, in addition to providing the founding principles of much of our lives, are also the foundations of the other two types of inventions: logical and physical. Conceptual inventions lead to logical inventions, which then can lead to physical inventions.

For instance, the conceptual invention of music led to logical inventions such as defining different tones and musical notes and the sequencing and duration of those notes. These logical inventions then led to the development of physical inventions such as sheet music, flutes, drums, CDs, and iPods.

If we didn't have the conceptual invention of music, we would very likely not need an iPod. Even more important to understand is that without the concept of music, an iPod would likely have little transformative value.

Figure 1.5 depicts how inventions evolve from conceptual into logical and finally into physical inventions. As depicted in the figure, the concept of project management created the logical process of utilizing a Gantt chart. This usage of Gantt charts eventually led to the creation of physical inventions such as Microsoft Project in order to simplify and automate much of the previous logical process. All three (project management, Gantt charts, and Microsoft Project) could each be termed innovative based on their individual degree of transformative impact and value.

Once a logical or physical invention evolves into product form, it is then often referred to as a business or technical invention. The distinction of

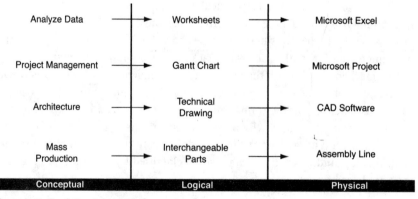

FIGURE 1.5 Evolving inventions

whether a product is a business invention, a technical invention, or both is often a seemingly arbitrary assignment.

Examples of logical inventions that would be viewed as business inventions include areas such as management styles, governance, and decision-making processes.

However, not all logical inventions are considered business inventions. For example, a new way of assembling computer circuits would be designated a technical invention.

The concept of analyzing and manipulating information can be greatly simplified by the utilization of a worksheet to arrange the information in an easy-to-view, logical manner. Prior to 1979, this process was largely manual and tedious. It would have been called a business process. The manual processes of utilizing a worksheet were then automated with the invention of physical inventions such as VisiCalc and Microsoft Excel. These physical inventions are still called business inventions since they deliver the same business processes that could be performed manually. However, they are also called technical inventions because they utilized new technologies, such as the data cell structure, to deliver business process improvement.

Figure 1.6 shows how inventions can be technical inventions, business inventions, or both. In addition, all of these inventions can potentially be product inventions.

The following chapters utilize extensively the definitions of different types of inventions and will define when it is critical for you to distinguish between the various types. The goal of delineating these invention types is to eliminate

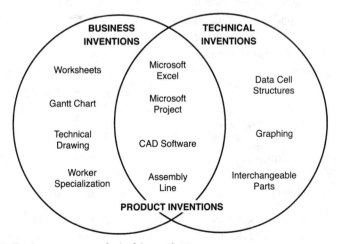

FIGURE 1.6 Business versus technical inventions

the randomness of existing invention and innovation processes by understanding the types of inventions required or utilized in a particular situation.

Internal and External Inventions

All companies have to perform a balancing act when it comes to the budget allocations for developing and/or deploying new inventions. When an invention is productized and deployed, either it can constitute an internal deployment that primarily impacts internal company processes, or it can be an external deployment in the form of a customer-utilized product. All too often, companies will realign their budgets to favor internal inventions and will not keep a reasonable balance of external versus internal invention.

Internal inventions are those where the transformative value of deploying the invention primarily benefits the company. Conversely, external inventions exhibit a transformative value that benefits the customer.

As illustrated in Figure 1.7, budgets shift toward internal invention because of three overriding drivers:

- **Cost reduction:** Cost reduction is the easiest to understand since the only way to reduce costs is through internal changes such as process improvements, staff reductions, and sales commission modifications.

- **Infrastructure investments:** Infrastructure investments can be viewed in two ways. First, legacy infrastructure costs may reduce external invention flexibility and drive invention budgets toward internal

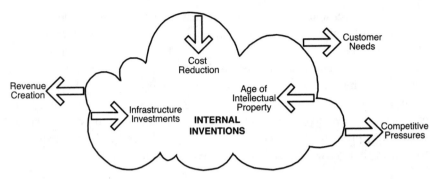

FIGURE 1.7 Internal versus external innovation

inventions. Second, new external inventions may force new infrastructure investments for productivity gains and again drive budgets toward internal invention.

- **Age of intellectual property**: As existing company inventions age, they will most likely become less competitive. This aging demands a continued investment in external invention. If external invention is ignored for too long, the costs of becoming competitive again through new external invention may become too great, forcing budgets toward internal invention.

Internal invention is the pursuit of new inventions that will enhance the business processes that a company currently has in place. Internal inventions can be business inventions such as job sharing, cross-training, offshoring, or outsourcing. Internal inventions could also be technical inventions such as data-center consolidation or process automation.

Figure 1.7 also points out the three overriding drivers that tend to push budgets toward external invention:

- **Revenue creation**: The continuous need to increase annual revenues is a major driver of budgets oriented toward external invention.

- **Customer needs**: Existing customers expect annual enhancements to products in order to justify their annual payments or purchases.

- **Competitive pressures**: As markets age, the number of competitors will normally increase, and product features will begin to commoditize. This commoditization lowers the value of existing external inventions and drives budgets toward new external invention.

External invention is the pursuit of new inventions that have a direct impact on the business or personal lifestyles of the company's customers. These would include any invention that tends to maintain competitive position or that extends competitive position through either enhancements to existing features or creation of entirely new markets.

As we will see later, as a company ages, it will shift its innovation from external to internal and inadvertently exposes the company to ever-increasing competitive pressures and eventual irrelevancy as others produce transformative value that causes its products to be leapfrogged.

Bob Should Consider

- What are the company's current circumstances that require more focus on either internal or external invention?
- Are we focusing too much budget on external invention that could create an opportunity for a low-cost competitor to displace us?
- Are we focusing too much budget on internal invention and cost reduction that could cause us to fall behind in delivering transformative value to our customers?
- What is the age of our intellectual property, and does it need to be refreshed?
- Have we examined the possibility of a new external invention being brought to market by ourselves or our competition that could change our market position?

Disruptive Innovation

We have discussed the concept of transformative value as a gauge of the innovativeness of a deployed product. A new product with little or no transformative value would not be considered beneficial to the company and, as we shall see shortly, can actually damage or destroy a company's competitive position.

A new product or feature that delivers a very large transformative value is often described as a disruptive innovation. Disruptive innovations create a significant change and/or improvement in the business or personal lifestyles of the innovation's consumers. The best way to view disruptive innovations is to consider them market makers and market changers.

Companies that deliver a product with disruptive innovations will often quickly become the dominant player within their market. The company may also own the key intellectual property needed to maintain the market dominant position for quite some time.

Disruptive innovations are most often delivered by new companies. Unlike older companies, new companies rarely have the overriding drivers that we discussed previously that will force budgets toward internal invention: cost reduction, existing infrastructure investments, and age of intellectual property. The lack of these internal invention pressures allows the new company to be driven by pressures that force external invention.

However, new companies are often under even greater revenue pressures than old companies and therefore will target their external inventions into very specific, targeted areas. It is this targeting of external inventions, discussed later, that is so critical to finding disruptive innovations. In most cases, the very fact that the new company was founded on a single, specific invention is the reason that a disruptive innovation came into being at all.

Google disrupted the Internet web search market with its new search engine. The Google founders started with a targeted, specific goal in mind: Create a better web search algorithm. But, when Google started making the algorithm available to the public for searching, there was no clearly defined method of creating revenue from that search process. It was only later that the Google search engine invention was wrapped within a second invention, an advertising auction invention, that a new way of earning revenue was created.

At the time of Google's introduction, Microsoft was one of the largest and most profitable companies in the world, and Microsoft controlled the search engine market through a multipronged product offering:

- Produced and monopolized the operating system running on virtually all PCs

- Developed and delivered the primary browser in use

- Created the Microsoft Network (MSN) to profit from consumers' connectivity and search activities

In spite of Microsoft's dominance and virtual control of the search engine market at the time of Google's arrival on the scene, Google now controls more than 75% of the search/advertising market and garnishes almost 90% of all new growth in the market. Google ripped the market away from Microsoft by creating a tool that did the following:

- Was easy to use

- More effectively found websites based on search queries

- Delivered a wider variety of content

- Returned search results much faster

- Successfully monetized the search process

In addition, Google out-marketed Microsoft by more effectively hyping its own technology and by turning the corporate name into a verb, as in "to Google." Google took its invention and through effective marketing highlighted the impact on consumer lifestyles and created a highly disruptive innovation with a huge transformative value.

Figure 1.8 shows a sampling of disruptive innovations, the market they were targeted at, and the lifestyle impact they delivered. For instance, the Apple iPod seized the portable media market in 2004 from Sony though the latter controlled the following:

- Sony Walkman and Sony Discman

- Contracts with leading music artists

- Half ownership of Sony BMG music, the world's largest independent music publisher

Innovation	Market	Lifestyle Impact
Amazon Kindle	E-books	Size, Battery Life, Wireless Network, Storage Capacity, Ease of Use
iPhone	Mobile Phone	Flexibility, Ease of Use, Expansion
Jelly Belly	Candy	Variety, Personalization, Gourmet
Text Messaging	Mobile Phone	Socializing, Nonverbal, Content
iPod	Portable Media Player	Size, Battery Life, PC Integration, Different Media, Storage Capacity
Instant Coffee	Beverage	Time, Shelf Life
Seat Belts	Safety Harness	Reduce Injuries, Save Lives

FIGURE 1.8 Disruptive innovations and lifestyle impact

Apple disrupted the market by introducing a completely new form of portable player that had huge impacts on consumer lifestyles and greatly exceeded the ease of use of existing products.

Apple and the iPod offerings are an example of an existing company entering a completely new and different market, creating a disruptive innovation, and causing a complete shift in the portable media player market.

Disruptive innovations can have a direct, disruptive impact on existing markets. Figure 1.9 shows how some products have impacted existing markets and/or created new markets.

BOB SHOULD CONSIDER

- Have we examined the transformative value of each of our external inventions to determine whether we are maximizing our ability to create disruptive innovations?

- Do our competitors possess external inventions that they could deploy to create disruptive innovations and thereby damage our market position? How do we anticipate and plan for this?

- How does the transformative value of each of our competitors products compare to our own products? How can we adjust this in our favor?

- How can we ensure that we are constantly performing like a "new" company? What markets that we are not in now might be advantageous for us to be disruptive in?

- Are we targeting our budgets for external inventions that maximize transformative value?

Innovation	Market	Market Impacts
Amazon Kindle	E-books	Accelerated Commoditization of Printed Books Market Established Viability of E-book Market
iPhone	Mobile Phone	Accelerated Commoditization of Key Pad Cell Phones Created Multitouch Cell Phone Market
Jelly Belly	Candy	Disrupted Jelly Bean Market
Text Messaging	Mobile Phone	Commoditized Mobile E-mail Market Created Mobile Text Messaging Market
iPod	Portable Media Player	Commoditized Portable CD Player Market Disrupted Portable Digital Player Market

FIGURE 1.9 Disruptive innovations and market impact

Incremental Innovation

Unlike disruptive innovations that have a large transformative impact, incremental innovations are delivered by inventions that do not cause a major shift in an existing market or create a new market. Incremental inventions/innovations have a much smaller transformative impact by adding features to an existing product or process that were originated by a previous disruptive innovation.

Incremental innovations can improve competitive positioning for the company that is delivering the incremental invention and may increase the company's market share and revenues. Consumers would look upon these types of incremental inventions as positive innovations and may be willing to pay an increased price to obtain them. For instance, expanding the storage capacity of an Apple iPod from 1GB to 30GB would be considered a positive incremental innovation.

One of the problems associated with repeated delivery of incremental inventions is that as new incremental inventions are delivered for an existing product, the product often increases in complexity. At a certain point, this increase in complexity may overshadow the perceived transformative value of the incremental invention. The new incremental invention would then be looked upon as an invention with a negative transformative value by the consumer, and the consumer would not be likely to accept increased costs for the invention.

This imbalance between complexity and feature density has been very evident in the case of the cellular phone market. The majority of consumers rarely use more than 10% of the functionality available in a standard mobile phone. In addition, approximately 60% of the functions are rarely ever utilized by consumers.

The majority of companies, driven by external invention pressures such as the need to increase revenues, will invariably begin to deliver negative incremental inventions unless they embark upon a path to instead deliver a new disruptive innovation.

Figure 1.10 describes different types of incremental inventions, the market they were targeted at, the perceived lifestyle impact, and whether the actual transformative value is considered to be positive or negative. As an example, the Amazon Kindle 2 product added new features including text to speech and an extended battery life. These new incremental invention's features allowed consumers to listen to books as well as read them and to do so for longer periods of time. The Kindle 2 constitutes an obvious positive incremental innovation within the e-books market.

Innovation	Market	Lifestyle Impact	Perceived Value
Amazon Kindle 2	E-books	Text to Speech, Capacity Increase, Extended Battery Life	Positive
iPhone 3G	Mobile Phone	Faster Communication, Assisted GPS	Positive
Increased Features	Mobile Phone	Poor Ergonomics, Confusing to Use	Negative
T9	Text Messaging	Predictive Text Messaging, Speed, Customizable	Positive
Microsoft Windows Vista	Operating System	High System Requirements, Expensive, Major GUI Shift	Negative

FIGURE 1.10 Incremental innovations and lifestyle impact

Conversely, the Microsoft Vista operating system can be looked upon as a negative incremental invention. Although it delivers better security features than previous versions of Windows, it does so with significant negative lifestyle impacts including increased system requirements, increased base pricing, and increased deployment complexity. In addition, the new, advanced graphical user interface (GUI) is a major shift from the traditional Windows GUI. The majority of the Windows consumer space has utilized the traditional Windows GUI for a long time. The overall learning curve to shift from Windows XP to Windows Vista is therefore perceived to be quite large. Becoming just as equally proficient, let alone more proficient, appears to the potential consumer to be a daunting and time-consuming task. This perceived complexity, in spite of an increased number of valuable features, caused Windows Vista to have a negative transformative value and led to consumers avoiding Vista.

Examples of incremental inventions in the PC computer market would consist of developments such as USB ports, wireless connectivity, enhanced sound and graphics systems, CD and DVD drives, and so on.

Although not necessarily disruptive in their respective markets, some incremental inventions have been disruptive innovations when viewed relative to completely different markets. As an example, providing computers with enhanced audio systems led to decreased sales of stand-alone stereos resulting in a disruption in the stereo market. Similarly, inclusion of internal CD and DVD drives in computers led to a disruption of the market for external CD and DVD players. Thus, it is important to realize that market disruptions can arise from innovations in completely different markets even if those innovations are not considered disruptive within their target markets.

Incremental inventions evolve a market through positive innovations but will eventually drive a product to commoditization through negative inventions. In some cases, negative incremental inventions can be destructive to the product and the market. Microsoft Vista borders closely on becoming a destructive invention. Microsoft recognized this and rushed Windows 7 to market in an attempt to stabilize its market image and positioning.

BOB SHOULD CONSIDER

- Are we focusing too much of our budget on incremental inventions instead of disruptive inventions?

- Will our incremental inventions be perceived as positive, negative, or destructive?

- How can we maximize delivery of positive incremental inventions while minimizing increases in product complexity?

- Are destructive inventions evident in our market, and does this reflect pending commoditization of the market?

- How can we utilize a competitor's products as guides to new disruptive inventions?

Destructive Invention

As companies continue to create new incremental inventions to maintain revenue streams and respond to external invention pressures, they run an ever-increasing risk of generating destructive inventions. A destructive invention is one that increases complexity rather than reducing it or that alienates existing customers in some way. A destructive invention not only is perceived to have a negative transformative value, but in addition, it causes the transformative value of prior deployed inventions to decrease as well.

Figure 1.11 shows several very costly inventions that damaged the consumer's perception of the company's products and resulted in a completely opposite impact from that sought by the company.

Destructive inventions are the best sign that a market is commoditizing or has already commoditized.

Invention	Market	Market Impact
Coca-Cola New Coke	Soft Drink	Alienated Loyal Drinkers
McDonald's Arch Deluxe	Fast Food	Expensive, Damaged Existing Branding, Negative Advertising
Automatic Passive Seat Belts	Safety Harness	Interfere with Vehicle Access, Not Compatible with Airbags and Child Safety Seats

FIGURE 1.11 Destructive inventions and market impact

BOB SHOULD CONSIDER

- Is there a way to induce our competitors to deliver destructive inventions that result in a more positive perception of our own products?
- Are we reviewing in sufficient detail the costs and risks experienced by our customers with each new incremental invention so that we can understand the lines between positive, negative, and destructive incremental inventions?
- If we are seeing responses to new incremental inventions that appear to value them negatively or destructively, how do we need to change our budgets and invention targets?

Good Enough Innovation

One of the most frequent mistakes that large, legacy companies make is to chase the largest customers to the complete exclusion of smaller customers. At first glance, this seems to be a sound business strategy since the largest customers generally provide larger individual revenue streams and reduce the overall customer support and product maintenance problems.

In the long run, however, ignoring the smaller customers creates the perfect opportunity for new competitors to enter the market with more streamlined and modern product offerings that, while not providing all the current functionality available to the larger enterprises, provide a solution that is "good enough" for small to medium enterprises. In addition, the products offered by these new competitors can often be evolved to move up the customer stack significantly easier than the legacy company can evolve their products to move back down the customer stack.

Newer competitors will function much like start-ups as far as the overriding pressures that drive internal versus external invention and are therefore far more targeted in their inventions and innovations. This start-up mentality gives the new competitors a much greater possibility of creating the next disruptive innovation and stealing market share from the legacy company.

For example, the extremely capable software packages sold by companies such as Oracle are normally too highly priced and overly complex to meet the more straightforward needs of small to medium enterprises. Although the Oracle packages may have a great deal of functionality, they exhibit a very low transformative value to small to medium enterprises. As of this writing, Oracle is attempting to reverse this trend by delivering less complex and less costly versions of its software products, which Oracle has branded Fusion, that are targeted at small to medium enterprises.

As we discussed earlier, incremental inventions are normally layered on top of products and services that came about through an earlier disruptive innovation. Repeated additions of new incremental inventions drive the product further and further away from the "good enough" version by repetitively increasing the price and product complexity while lowering the transformative value.

The danger for the incumbent company is that the new "good enough" providers will reset the level of functionality that is considered good enough not only for small to medium enterprises but for larger enterprises as well. This resetting of "good enough" functionality acts as a new disruptive innovation within the market. This disruption effectively shifts control of the evolution of the market away from the incumbent and toward the newer competitor. The surprising thing is that an evaluation of market share and sales volumes will often not reflect that this shift in market evolution control has occurred, often for quite some time.

As we will discuss later in this book, there are ways for the incumbent to maximize its dominant position in the market and to reset the disruptive innovation level without increasing risk. We will also discuss how the newer product providers can utilize the dominant incumbent's position to the new provider's advantage.

BOB SHOULD CONSIDER

- Has a new competitor effectively reset the "good enough" level of functionality within our market and stolen control of the evolution of the market?

- Are we ignoring small to medium enterprises and providing opportunities for more aggressive competitors to seize our market position?
- How can we utilize our market position to protect ourselves from new entrants?
- How can we anticipate attacks from new entrants and remain dominant?
- How can we balance our internal and external invention pressures to more effectively compete against new market entrants?
- In spite of market sales figures, have we already reset the control of market evolution to our advantage? Are we taking advantage of our new position?
- Have we examined what is considered to be "good enough" by our customers, and are we lowering our value by exceeding that level?

Targeted Invention and Innovation

We have discussed many types of inventions and innovations. All of these types of inventions and innovations must be reflected within any working invention and innovation process if we are to minimize risk and maximize potential success. Surprisingly, few of these types of inventions and innovations are reflected in the innovation practices taught and implemented today:

- Increase the number of inventors.
- Increase the odds of recognizing a potentially viable invention by training management and implementing more flexible policies.
- Increase the number of attempts the company hunts for innovations by deploying more new inventions through the increased taking of risk by executive management.

The one area of invention that is almost universally overlooked is targeted invention. Targeted invention is the type of invention that gave birth to Microsoft through the DOS operating system, the birth of Google through a new search engine, and the birth of Apple through the personal computer. Apple later expanded the company's successes through targeted invention of the iPod and the iPhone.

Currently taught innovation rules and practices are a response to the perceived randomness of finding and developing new disruptive innovations. As we will see later, these rules and practices can actually increase the randomness of the innovation process and decrease the probability of a company succeeding.

Successful start-up companies understand the concept of targeted invention extremely well. They are driven by the need to invent a solution for a particular market need. They are not driven by stockholder demands for increased revenues, customer demands for increased features, or infrastructure expense pressures. They remain focused on the need to create a targeted invention for a targeted market need. Like Google did, they largely ignore the marketing requirements and the innovation path until they have completed the invention process.

Many disruptive, innovative products and companies are "built in a garage" and "started on a shoestring." Why can't existing companies create disruptive innovations with minimal risk and minimal cash outlay and avoid the expansion of management layers? They can—but rarely by following the current innovation rules/practices.

In later chapters, we will discuss in great detail how to implement targeted invention and innovation within your company without the need to follow the currently taught three innovation rules.

BOB SHOULD CONSIDER

- What are our invention and innovation targets?
- Can we understand our competitors' invention and innovation road maps and beat them to their defined targets?
- Are we considering all the types of inventions and innovations in our processes, or are we locked into the underlying assumption of randomness?

Impact of Consumption Priorities

It is critical to understand the ways that a consumer may perceive and value a new product. It is equally important to understand the external pressures, unrelated to the actual product, that also impact a consumer's decision to buy a new product. At a high level, these external pressures are time, money, and lifestyle. Digging a little deeper gets us to what a consumer considers most important: the consumer's consumption priorities.

Examples of consumption priorities surround us. Hard-core gamers buy expensive, high-end gaming equipment and spend a large majority of their free time gaming. Sports people buy season tickets as well as all the broadcast sports that their money can acquire. To those of us who might not share these same consumption priorities, these would seem to be odd ways to spend one's money. But, each of us has one or more consumption priorities that we indulge in. These can be as diverse as eating expensive granola, wearing and owning a lot of beautiful shoes, or listening to jazz music and going to jazz concerts.

Sometimes these consumption priorities are easily defined addictions such as smoking or drinking. Perhaps all of the other cravings that we have including eating gourmet chocolates, drinking energy shakes, or reading all the books of a favorite author should also be categorized as addictions. Just like beauty, the value of each of our consumption priorities is in the eye of the beholder. A pepperoni pizza could easily constitute a consumption priority for many consumers. My personal consumption priority is eating Asian foods.

In many cases, these consumption priorities are the little luxuries in our lives that we think we deserve almost at any cost. This deep degree of attachment to our consumption priorities makes it critical that when a company is considering bringing a new product to market, the company understands the consumption priorities of the product's potential consumers. These consumption priorities will often dictate and potentially limit the overall perceived value of the new product in the eyes of the consumer. Let's discuss three ways to maximize the impact of people's consumption priorities toward delivering a recognizable product innovation.

First, new products can be targeted directly in an existing market for a product that is a consumption priority, such as the chocolate market. Companies attempting to deliver these new products must ensure that the product's perceived value exceeds existing products in that market. Otherwise, the product will not be perceived as innovative and at best will be perceived as competitive with existing products.

Simply introducing another brand of dark chocolate is not likely to induce any form of market disruptions. But, introducing flavorings that can be sprinkled on dark chocolate and then eaten has a different potential. This allows the individual consumer to create an almost limitless variety of unique-flavored chocolate sensations that fit with that consumer's favorite tastes. A product that maximizes, on an individual consumer basis, the perceived value for each consumer within a consumption priority market has the potential to create quite a stir within that market and become a true innovation.

Second, a product can be directed at a market that consists of products that are considered to be more "common" in nature and is therefore not a consumption priority market. If the product does not create a new consumption priority market, then the product will likely have a relatively standard perceived value for products in that market. This standard perceived value makes it critical that the new product increase the value to the consumer in other ways. The easiest way to do this is by impacting the ability of consumers to enjoy their lifestyles, regardless of what their lifestyle priorities might be.

The third manner of utilizing consumer consumption priorities for maximum product innovation potential is to introduce a new product that creates a new consumption priority market and in the process may eliminate an existing consumption priority market. The consumer is unlikely to see the perceived value of the new product and unlikely to switch to the new product's consumption priority market unless there are positive impacts on the consumer's personal or business lifestyle.

Let's consider an example using coffee. People who drink coffee are drinking hot, naturally flavored water that they then further flavor to taste by adding sugar, cream, and additional flavorings. A company could introduce "new coffee" that is an artificial version of coffee. This drink would likely be much cheaper to produce and therefore to sell. The "new coffee" drink, when heated, would deliver the same drinking sensation as regular coffee does for the legacy coffee drinker. However, to get the consumer to switch to the new product, the new product would probably have to be priced significantly lower than regular coffee or in some other way enhance the consumer's lifestyle. Otherwise, the consumer would be unlikely to switch.

Bob Should Consider

- Is our product perceived as a consumption priority, and are we maximizing our value to those consumers?

- If our product is not a consumption priority, can we enhance our product in such a way that it indirectly increases the perceived value of our product to consumers and becomes a consumption priority?

everyone acknowledges as the best burger around, your business will probably fail. This is because the transformative value from the company's viewpoint is vastly different from the viewpoint of the target consumer.

BOB SHOULD CONSIDER

- Are we viewing our product purely from the perceived value point of view or from the broader transformative value viewpoint?
- Have we made assumptions about our target market without considering all aspects of perceived value, consumption priorities, and lifestyle priorities?
- If our product is targeted at multiple markets, have we considered the differences between the transformative values for the multiple markets?
- Is our sales and marketing plan optimized for our consumer's viewpoint, and is our projected transformative value utilizing that viewpoint?

Trigger Points

The point at which a potential consumer becomes an actual consumer of a product can be defined as a **trigger point.** Individuals within a target market have their own unique level at which they will decide to proceed with or abandon a purchase. It is the manufacturer's job to maximize the number of consumers who reach their trigger point. This average trigger point is a reflection of the transformative value of the product.

Within any target market, there will always be consumers who, regardless of a product having a high transformative value, will still refrain from purchasing the product. There may be any number of reasons why a consumer will never reach a trigger point with regard to a particular product. Sometimes, there just is no overriding requirement for the product even though it could help satisfy a lifestyle priority. These are the cases where companies do everything in their power to close the sale the first time; otherwise, the sale will likely never occur.

"Absolutely free" is a tag line that is often used to try to shift the transformative value of a product. How many times have you seen it on a sign, web page, or advertisement? And yet, you did not proceed. Many of us have a built-in barrier that declares "nothing is free," and unless the transformative value is extremely high, we are unwilling to take the risk of acquiring something that is absolutely free. In other words, the potential for negative lifestyle impact is too great for us to move forward.

This apparent disjointedness between marketing attempts and marketing effectiveness indicates that there are actually two different transformative values involved. The first is the one defined by the company selling the product. The second is the one defined by the target consumer. In the cases where the consumer clicked the "absolutely free" link, the company marketing the product may have done a good job of balancing these two transformative values for the consumer's trigger point. In cases where the consumer did not click the link, the consumer did not reach a trigger point that satisfied the transformative value.

Bob Should Consider

- Have we evaluated our target consumers enough to understand their purchase trigger point?

- Does our assumed transformative value match the transformative value from our target consumer's point of view?

- Do we have indications from our marketing and sales that our assumed transformative value is incorrect? Are targeted consumers responding the way we expected?

- How can we adjust our marketing methods to decrease our target, a consumer's trigger point, to be more in line with our calculated transformative value?

- How can we adjust our marketing methods to increase consumers' overall perceived transformative value and reach their trigger points?

Early Adopters

Early adopters are an example of consumers who have a very low trigger point. They will purchase the product even if the perceived value for other potential consumers is not optimal. What is important to understand about early adopters is that their purchase does reflect their consumption or lifestyle priorities. They are the electronic geeks, cooking fanatics, or any number of other categories of individuals. They would consider being branded with the category label as a compliment.

Even though the new product may come to market with a low transformative value because of flaws in the initial release or design, the early adopter will override these imperfections and view the product as if it had a much higher transformative value. This apparent dynamic shifting in consumer acceptance of a product in spite of an initially low perceived value is a clear indication that the product is a consumption or lifestyle priority.

When a company is considering deploying a new product, especially if the product is deploying into a new market, the company should create two separate transformative values. The first transformative value should reflect the different lifestyle priorities of the early adopter within the target consumer base. The second transformative value reflects the lifestyle priorities of the average target consumer.

By targeting the early adopters, the company is gaining a critical and yet easily obtained market foothold. Since the trigger point for the early adopter reflects a lower transformative value, almost any properly targeted product will garnish an initial market share.

In addition, early adopters are the tuning forks of a new product's transformative value. Feedback from early adopters is critical to properly fine-tuning the transformative value for the larger consumer base. Their feedback helps correct product issues that lower the perceived value and that define ways in which the product can impact consumer business and personal lifestyle priorities. Further, as other consumers see their early adopter friends use the new product, the product will increase its transformative value for the average target consumer with increased sales as those trigger points are reached.

BOB SHOULD CONSIDER

- Have we identified the lifestyle priorities that define our product's early adopters?

- Are we staging our product to maximize the number of early adopters and enhance our market and consumer learning curve? Are our marketing efforts designed to maximize early adopter contact and feedback?

- Can we adjust our product so as to utilize the early adopters' feedback and thereby adjust our overall market transformative value?

- How do we ensure that early adopters are able to help us market our product to average consumers and positively impact the perception of our broader transformative value?

3

The Innovation Life Cycle

Now that we know about ideas and the transformative value process necessary to decide whether those ideas should be dismissed, are worthy of becoming inventions, or maybe even are innovations, it's time to understand in more detail the types of innovation and the life cycle that innovation takes. This is important since where our idea falls in the life cycle will determine how we need to think about the idea and what next steps we take to maximize the value of the idea.

Yes, ideas that are successful (or even some that are not) do go through a life cycle. It can be that the idea is so new and radical that it is a new innovation and must go through all of the growing pains and excitement of initial innovation that then disrupts the marketplace.

It's possible that the idea, although quite innovative, is more of an add-on to an existing idea and better thought of as incremental innovation. Such incremental innovation usually starts out as positive but, when continued too long, can frequently end up as negative and ultimately destructive.

How can one tell where "positive" ends and "negative" starts? The key is the concept of **inflection points** in thinking about ideas and where they potentially fall. A knowledge of these concepts will keep the astute reader on the path of the optimal innovation life cycle. It's important to know when you are throwing good money after bad, especially when you can be putting that good money into the next disruptive innovation!

Innovation Types

To provide a foundation for the book, Chapter 1 presented many types of invention and innovation. In total, six distinct types of innovation are discussed in this book, and they can be grouped into four categories:

- Innovations that evolve a product and impact the perceived value of the product:
  - **Disruptive innovation**: A new product that creates a shift in an existing market or creates a new market
  - **Incremental innovation**: Something that adds new value to an existing foundational product that was created by a previous disruptive innovation
- Innovations that define how a company chooses to spend its invention innovation budget:
  - **Internal innovation**: Invention and innovation that is directed internally within a company to deliver cost savings, process improvements, or other internal benefits
  - **External innovation**: Invention and innovation that is directed externally toward delivering product innovations to a consumer and a market
- Innovation that targets consumers whose lifestyle priorities do not justify the best product possible:
  - **Good enough innovation**: Creating a product offering that meets the reduced lifestyle priorities of a consumer subgroup
- Innovation that ensures that the target consumer and market are well understood before invention begins:
  - **Targeted innovation**: Clearly matching a company's business priorities with consumer priorities prior to product invention so as to maximize the transformative value of the product

The Innovation Life Cycle

The innovation life cycle tracks the life of a single product and consists of multiple invention and innovation stages. These stages reflect how a company's actions impact the target market for the product. Depicted in Figure 3.1, the innovation life cycle consists of the following stages:

1. **Product invention:** Create the foundational product.

2. **Disruptive innovation:** Market penetration of the new product with a high consumer transformative value takes place.

3. **Incremental invention:** Add functionality or features to the foundational product.

4. **Positive incremental innovation:** Enhance transformative value.

5. Repeat stages 3 to 5 until transformative value no longer increases.

6. **Negative incremental invention:** Add functionality or features to the foundational product beyond customer acceptance levels, leading to a decrease of the product's transformative value.

7. Repeat stage 6 until transformative value equals competitors in the market.

8. **Destructive invention:** Further invention accelerates the decrease of the transformative value.

BOB SHOULD CONSIDER

- How does this high-level definition of a product's innovation life cycle compare with our understanding?
- What stage of the innovation life cycle is our product in?
- Have we related our product development processes to the consumer's changing transformative value for our product?

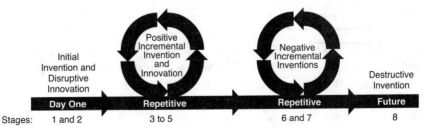

FIGURE 3.1 The innovation life cycle

Stage 1: Initial Invention

The development of a successful, innovative product is perceived by many to be a highly expensive, risky, and largely random process. While reviewing the innovation life cycle in detail, we will identify activities within the life cycle that are the cause of this perception of randomness. This accumulated perception of randomness will be discussed in detail in a later chapter.

The initial invention stage starts with identifying a perceived market need. This market need is often quantified by an evaluation of the consumer's perceived value for an invention (product) that could satisfy the identified need.

Many companies utilize a sampling of the potential market to determine the needs of the entire market. The percentage of the sample that exhibits each need is calculated. This percentage of needy consumers is then extrapolated to apply to the entire market. The result is a valuation for the projected total market size for needy customers. For reasons that will be explained shortly, this extrapolation of need injects the first appearance of randomness into the innovation process.

After identifying the market size, it is necessary to calculate the projected cost of delivering a product to satisfy the identified need. This cost is couched in various parameters related to the complexity of the product, development time, marketing expense, support requirements, and so on.

After calculating cost, it is optimal to calculate the product's perceived value to the consumer. The projected cost and the projected perceived value provide a means of comparison that is used to determine the worth of pursuing the invention process to create the new product.

Figure 3.2 graphically depicts the determination of the target market using market samples and perceived value. The figure shows that only a subset of consumers (the targeted area) will have a high enough perceived value to warrant the purchase of a product that fulfills the identified need.

Many companies would assume at this point that the perceived value is a reasonable reflection of the consumer's willingness to purchase the product. As discussed in previous chapters, it is critical that invention and innovation decisions be made based on the total transformative value, not just based on the perceived value.

In many cases, an in-depth market review will not have been performed prior to starting the product invention process. To really understand the impacts of the targeted consumer's consumption and lifestyle priorities on the perceived value, such a review is necessary and would help determine the transformative value of the product. As a result, the lack of definition of the transformative value provides the next point at which randomness is injected into the innovation process.

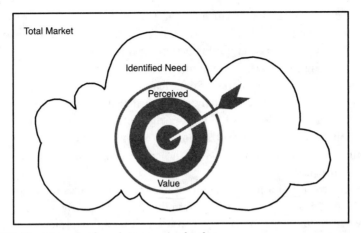

FIGURE 3.2 Target market based on perceived value

Figure 3.3 shows how the actual market for the product, when based on transformative value instead of perceived value as depicted in Figure 3.2, can be dramatically different.

At the initiation of an invention development process, we want to optimize the efforts of the development team for creating a product with high transformative value; that is, we want to maximize the size and value of the market that is willing to purchase. This requires utilizing a complete definition of the potential consumers based on a study of consumers' transformative value. Otherwise, the development team will be targeting the broader needs of the market and not the needs of the consumers who would be most interested in the product based on their lifestyle priorities. Without this focus, the probability is high

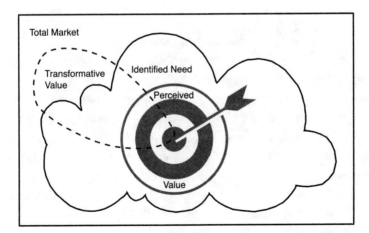

FIGURE 3.3 Actual market based on transformative value

that the development team will miss the feature/function target of the real market. By having too broad of a market definition, the invention development team injects the next perception of randomness into the innovation process.

Based on Figure 3.2, the development team will develop the invention relative to the entire target market. Some features may be dropped because of increased complexity or cost. If these dropped features push the product so that it is targeting primarily the bottom right of the target market, then the target will be missed. Figure 3.3 shows how the product could completely miss the functional requirements of the consumers who are most likely to purchase the product.

The incorrect definition of the target market also reduces the ability of the management team to accurately determine whether an invention, should it succeed in becoming a market innovation, will be an incremental or disruptive innovation. An invention that started out sounding like a market-dominating product could easily end up being a small niche product. The inability to properly project the success of a product by the management team injects more perceptions of randomness into the innovation life cycle. The increasing perception of randomness forces the management team to assume an increased level of risk in order to find a successful invention/innovation.

Many venture capital–backed start-ups fail to ever exit stage 1 of the innovation life cycle. The start-up may have a fabulous product, but the products are often poorly targeted because of an improperly identified market. In this instance, the created product delivers no increased transformative value to the targeted consumer since the targeted consumer is not the consumer who could benefit most from the product. Although the new product may be competitive, it will likely not be disruptive or even incremental to the market or the consumers.

BOB SHOULD CONSIDER

- When determining what products to build, how do we determine the market needs that we are trying to satisfy?

- Are we ensuring that those consumers with an identified need would also be willing to purchase the product at our projected price?

- Does our marketing team provide sufficient definition of the target consumer to guarantee that the development team will hit the right target?

- Before investing in the development of a new product, have we, whether as a management team or as a venture capital firm, properly identified the target consumers of the product and the transformative value of the product to those consumers?

and transformative value = Consumer's perceived need + consumer's lifestyle priorities

Stage 2: Disruptive Innovation

Once the foundational product has been created through invention in stage 1, it can be taken to market with the intention of creating an innovation in the consumer's eyes. The consumer will purchase the product only if the product has a high enough transformative value. The transformative value reflects the combination of a consumer's perceived value of the product as well as a consumer's lifestyle priorities, which may impact the decision to purchase.

A product newly introduced to the market that has a tremendously successful reception is many times a complete surprise to everyone involved. Although the developers may have anticipated a good reception for the product, becoming a disruptive force within the market is a fairly rare event. The inability to predict accurately whether a product will be merely a competitive product within the market or that the product will disrupt the market is yet another point at which the innovation process appears to have random properties.

Some innovations that appear initially to be disruptive can have extremely short lives in the market. These "disruptive innovation spikes" can be caused by the company having a marketing initiative that creates incorrect preconceptions in the mind of the consumer before the product rollout. In this case, there will be an initial rush to acquire the product. But, if the product subsequently fails to match up to the early adopters' predelivery expectations, the early adopters' transformative value for the product will quickly plummet, and word will soon get around to others who might have purchased. This situation can potentially damage the product's marketability beyond repair.

The incorrect consumer perception of the product could be an intentional overstatement of the product's capabilities and value by the product's marketing group. However, in many cases the apparent disjoint between what the company is saying and what the consumer is hearing is caused by the misalignment of the company's transformative value of the product with the consumer's actual transformative value for the product. As shown in Figure 3.4, if the marketing team presents the product's capabilities in terms of the product's perceived value, consumers may very well interpret these capabilities relative to their own personal lifestyle priorities. It is easy to visualize how the presentation of a broad picture of a product's capabilities can unintentionally expand the product's impact on a consumer's lifestyle priorities.

The occurrence of disruptive innovation spikes further expands the perceived randomness of the innovation process. Disruptive innovation spikes are also another reason that executive management teams think that delivering new products and pursuing disruptive innovations is extremely risky and unpredictable.

Company Marketing Based on Perceived Values		Consumer Lifestyle Priorities	Consumer Perception of Transformative Value
Faster		Family	Time
Superior		Work	Money
Flexible		Activities	Simplification

FIGURE 3.4 Causes of disruptive innovation spike

In some cases, companies will bring a product to market that is not disruptive at all. Such products are at best competitive with existing products. In these cases, the company, through its new product, is attempting to gain joint control of product innovation within the market. This joint control can be achieved by matching the foundational features of a product that was created through a competitor's disruptive innovation.

This market entry method is probably the most common because it has the least identifiable risk. The new competitor is counting on being more innovative in the future, at least incrementally, than the already dominant competition. The new product still passes through stage 2 of the innovation life cycle, but instead of creating its own disruption, the product benefits from the disruptive innovation of an already existing product.

BOB SHOULD CONSIDER

- Do we know whether our product should be disruptive to the market or merely competitive?
- If our product does not become a disruptive innovation, what are the risks that we face?
- Are we utilizing the disruptive product foundations of our competitors to maximize our ability to deliver an incremental innovation?
- Do we understand our target consumer well enough to market to them effectively? Are our marketing efforts presenting the best picture of our product by considering the true transformative values of our consumer?

Stage 3: Incremental Invention

After a company has succeeded in bringing to market a product that becomes a disruptive innovation, the natural tendency for the company is to expand the market disruption. Expansion of the market disruption will allow the company to control the evolution of the market. Incremental inventions evolve the existing product in ways that will ideally enhance the transformative value of the product and expand the target market.

Except in cases where a company has a very small number of customers, the odds are high that there will be features requested by some customers who are completely useless to other customers. Requests for new features submitted by larger customers will almost always be rolled into the product through incremental invention, potentially causing a negative experience for other, smaller customers.

As with the development efforts in stage 1 of the innovation life cycle, the development team that is creating incremental inventions must have a firm definition of the target consumer. Otherwise, poorly implemented incremental inventions can severely damage the product in the consumer's eyes.

The marketing team should also monitor the transformative value of the product as it is being evolved through incremental invention.

BOB SHOULD CONSIDER

- Are we optimally performing incremental invention in order to expand the market disruption caused by our product? Or have we missed this opportunity?
- Are we damaging our product in the eyes of some of our customers by focusing too much on the requests of larger customers? Can we balance the effect?
- Is our marketing team monitoring the impact of our incremental inventions and those of our competitors on our product's transformative value?

Stage 4: Positive Incremental Innovation

Each customer has different business priorities. This difference makes it highly likely that different customers will perceive each incremental invention from vastly different perspectives. Some customers will consider the incremental inventions as critical enhancements. Other customers will consider the incremental inventions as too complex, as unnecessary, or as too expensive. If a majority of customers, or at least the largest ones, consider the inventions to be valuable, then the transformative value of the product has been increased by the incremental inventions. This results in the inventions becoming incremental innovations.

In many ways, early incremental innovations can act as follow-on disruptive innovations to the primary disruptive innovation in stage 2. These follow-on disruptive innovations are similar to the aftershocks that follow earthquakes. Most of us would not consider an earthquake to be over until all of the aftershocks are gone. The same holds true for disruptive innovations followed by incremental innovations. If the incremental innovations continue to accelerate the dominance of the product in the market, then they are disruptive innovation aftershocks.

If, however, the incremental innovations do not continue to accelerate market dominance, in spite of being deemed as positive by the majority of existing customers and also increasing the transformative value of the product, then the disruptive innovation earthquake within the market has likely ended.

This abatement of the disruptive innovation aftershocks is the first innovation life cycle inflection point (inflection point A of Figure 3.5). At inflection point A, the company's new incremental inventions are just maintaining a competitive position for the product. Figure 3.5 shows the impact on market dominance when incremental invention shifts from delivering disruptive

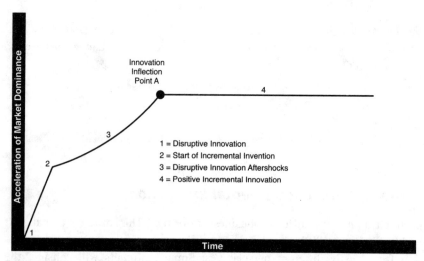

FIGURE 3.5 Disruptive innovation aftershocks

innovation aftershocks to incremental innovation. The market share may continue to grow, but the acceleration of that growth has ceased.

It is at innovation inflection point A that many companies begin to question their invention and innovation practices. There is a tendency to continue to fund product development on this existing product after inflection point A, even though the company is realizing decreasing returns to scale and quite possibly has better investment opportunities elsewhere. The management team likely does not realize that the transformative value of its product is constantly in flux. Incremental inventions can cause both positive and negative shifts in the transformative value of the product. Many of the fluctuations experienced with product sales are caused by the direct actions of the company and not by external forces. These direct actions will be discussed in later sections.

Inflection point A is also the first point where companies begin to shift resources from external to internal invention and innovation. At inflection point A, company executives see that the market growth is slowing. In response to this slowing, the team will seek to optimize internal infrastructures and to lower costs.

BOB SHOULD CONSIDER

- Are our incremental innovations acting as disruptive innovation aftershocks? How can we maximize this effect?
- Have we reached innovation inflection point A? What should our response be?
- How will we know whether our incremental inventions are now causing a negative shift in the transformative value of our product?

Stage 5: Repetitive Incremental Innovation

Approach any experienced software developers about two software products with which the developers are equally unfamiliar. One of the products is an older, stable, well-established product. The other product is newer with stability issues and slow market acceptance. Functionally, the products are very similar. Now ask the developers which product they would want to use as the foundation for creating a reduced-functionality "good enough" product. The preference for the developers will almost universally be to utilize the newer system. Not surprisingly, most management would pick the older system.

Why are the responses different between the developers and management? Management would select the older system because of external factors. The older system is more stable in the customers' eyes. The older system has had a lot of money, time, and manpower invested into it that has made it a market-accepted product. The older product is safer to use and is less likely to cause trouble for management.

Conversely, the developers choose the newer system because of internal factors. The newer system uses technology that is more interesting and that will look good on their resumes. It's a challenge for the developers to get the newer system to work, and that will also be interesting. As depicted in Figure 3.6, each time an incremental invention is added to the base disruptive product, the internals of the product become increasingly more complex. Externally, the product is improving. Internally, however, the product is becoming harder to expand, harder to maintain, and harder to evolve.

There are many well-known examples of software systems that exhibit staggering complexity brought on through years of incremental innovation. Two such software systems are those utilized by the U.S. Internal Revenue Service and the U.S. Federal Aviation Administration. In spite of making multibillion-dollar investments, both of these software platforms are so internally complex that replacing them with more stable platforms has so far proven almost impossible.

As incremental invention and innovation are repeated again and again to the same disruptive product foundation, multiple events begin to happen:

- The internal product complexity increases.

- The cost of new incremental invention/innovation increases.

- The cost of support and maintenance increases.

- The difficulty of evolving the product to new disruptive products increases.

- The customer satisfaction decreases.

- The customer willingness to fund incremental inventions decreases.

- The probability of a new simpler product arising from a competitor increases.

From the company's point of view, repetitive incremental invention complicates product development, sales, and support. But, incremental invention is the only way to continue to increase revenues from the product through increased billings to customers.

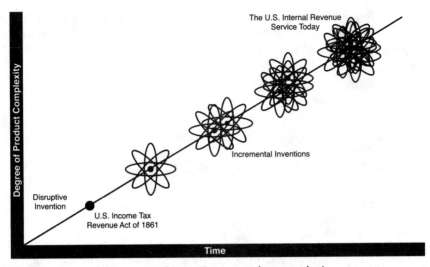

FIGURE 3.6 Impact of incremental invention on product complexity

From the consumer's viewpoint, repetitive incremental invention makes the product more difficult to understand and use and more expensive to acquire and maintain. Each time that an incremental invention/innovation passes through the innovation life cycle, the per-invention cost to the consumer is likely to increase.

BOB SHOULD CONSIDER

- How can we deploy new incremental inventions and innovations without continuously increasing the internal complexity of our product?

- Can we justify the costs of enforcing an internal product simplification policy? Are we considering the costs of future support, evolution, and maintenance?

- Is the rising complexity of our product increasing the cost of each new invention to the point that even our largest customers will complain?

Stage 6: Negative Incremental Invention

As revenues start to decrease because of a customer's unwillingness to bear the increasing costs for decreasing value, the company will start to shift away from external invention and innovation. Instead, the company will begin to focus on internal invention/innovation in a move to reduce costs. During stages 3 through 5 of the innovation life cycle, business pressures on the company have been increasingly shifting the company away from disruptive innovation and toward incremental innovation. These business pressures can be summarized as follows:

- **Revenue pressures**: Must increase revenue while decreasing risk
- **Customer pressures**: Need to satisfy existing, large customers through increased product features
- **Infrastructure pressures**: Need to ensure maximum utilization of existing infrastructure while decreasing costs

As we see in Figure 3.7, these business pressures suppress disruptive invention/innovation and increase incremental invention/innovation. Innovation inflection point B reflects a major change point for the product and the company. Multiple events are occurring at inflection point B (discussed in detail later), with one of the primary events being incremental invention surpassing disruptive invention.

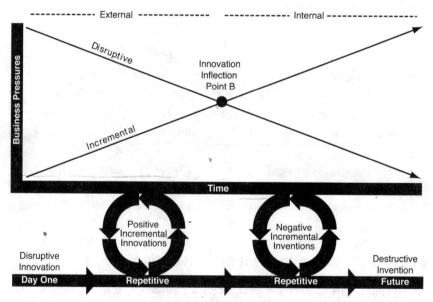

FIGURE 3.7 Impact of business pressures on innovation

Some of the actions that the company is likely to take at this inflection point include the following:

- Reduce the research and development budget
- Seek research and development alignments with the largest customers
- Increase the rate of internal infrastructure evolution
- Seek new markets and products through mergers and acquisitions
- Reduce or move the executive management team to the next product

These changes are brought on primarily by the decreasing revenues from the foundational product innovation. Each negative incremental invention tends to decrease the transformative value of the product and thereby reduce the competitiveness of the product.

BOB SHOULD CONSIDER

- Are our actions that impact our product driven increasingly by perceived business pressures that are not optimal for the positioning of the product in the market?
- As we shift in response to reaching innovation life cycle inflection point B, are we effectively "sealing the fate" of our product?
- In seeking short-term revenues through incremental inventions, some of which will negatively impact the long-term transformative value of the product, are we killing the long-term revenue potential of the product?

Stage 7: Repetitive Negative Incremental Invention

The company will likely accelerate the rate of product incremental invention in an attempt to regain revenue growth and maintain market competitiveness. However, the ever-increasing complexity of the product and the rising per-invention cost will limit the acceptability of most of these new incremental inventions. At innovation inflection point B, as depicted in Figure 3.8, new incremental inventions start to have an accelerating negative effect on the product and its transformative value. New incremental inventions are no longer perceived as innovations.

Not surprisingly, customers are following their own innovation life cycles relative to the deployment of the product within their internal infrastructure.

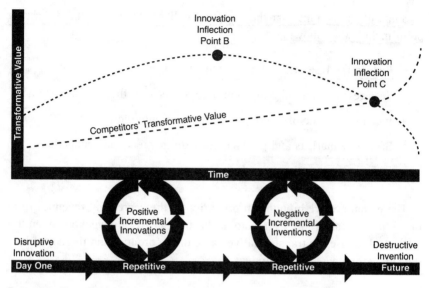

FIGURE 3.8 Transformative value throughout the innovation life cycle

These customers are continuously adjusting their calculations of the transformative value of the product relative to the transformative value of the product's competitors. As shown in Figure 3.8, innovation inflection point C coincides with the point that the product's transformative value no longer exceeds that of the competition.

As the transformative value approaches and passes inflection point C, the product's larger customers will continue to utilize the product. Cost of replacement for the larger customers is a large inhibitor to change and can artificially inflate their perceived transformative value of the evolving product. But, this artificial inflation of the transformative value will not sustain itself, and even the large customers will begin evaluating a replacement strategy.

Smaller customers, with lower costs of replacement, will begin to shift to simpler competitive products as the product's complexity begins to outweigh the product's feature set. It is at inflection point C that many customers begin to pursue an alternative "good enough" product.

BOB SHOULD CONSIDER

- Have we considered the innovation life cycle that our customers are following relative to our product? How can we use this information to maximize customer satisfaction and retention?

The Optimal Innovation Life Cycle

As we have seen, the current innovation life cycle (Figure 3.1) has some serious shortcomings. Increasing business pressures and the perceived market changes at the innovation inflection points will force the executive management team to make decisions that minimize risk and maximize return from the existing product and internal infrastructure.

Figure 3.10 depicts the optimal innovation life cycle. By proper management throughout this optimal innovation life cycle, it is possible to avoid the landslide effect of the previously described innovation inflection points. We will discuss how to implement the optimal innovation life cycle and how to utilize it to your company's advantage in later chapters.

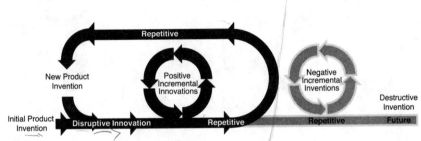

FIGURE 3.10 The optimal innovation life cycle

PART II
Business and Technical Life Cycles

4

Business Life Cycles

T o have a complete and nuanced view of innovation, it is necessary to understand and be able to use a variety of business life cycles. The product life cycle represents the consumer's view of the product. The market life cycle represents the view from the perspective of the various competitors within a market for a specific product. The company life cycle represents the view from the perspective of the corporate executives within a company delivering a product. How these life cycles work, and their relationship to each other as well as the innovation life cycle discussed in previous chapters, is the focus of this chapter.

Business Life Cycles

There are probably thousands of different ways to view how a product is developed, sold, deployed, and supported. To simplify matters, this book will present four different views in the form of business life cycles. The innovation life cycle was the first business life cycle and was presented in Chapter 3.

Of the four business life cycles, there are two internal life cycles. In this case, the term *internal* refers to inside a company. These internal life cycles are as follows:

- **The innovation life cycle:** The view from the perspective of the product development team and the company overall

- **The company life cycle:** The view from the perspective of the executive and management teams

There are also two external business life cycle views. The term *external* refers to outside the company that owns the internal life cycles. These external life cycles are as follows:

- **The product life cycle:** The view from the perspective of the customer
- **The market life cycle:** The view from the perspective of competitors

There are many benefits to understanding these four different views and having a firm definition for each life cycle. Some of the key benefits are as follows:

- The life cycles provide us with a means of understanding why companies make the business decisions that they do.
- We can see the impacts of our decisions within one life cycle on the other life cycles. For instance, changing actions within the innovation life cycle will impact the customer and the market, as well as executive decisions.
- We can deduce where our competitors are within their life cycles. We can use this information to our benefit, which allows us to compete more effectively.
- Our products can be targeted to maximize the transformative value to our customers.
- We can avoid or at least minimize the negative stages that are inherent in each of the life cycles.

Figure 4.1 depicts the four different business views.

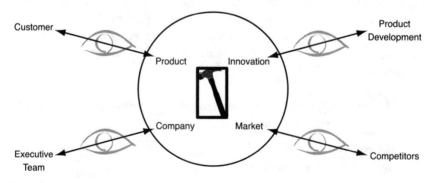

FIGURE 4.1 Business life cycle views

Product Life Cycle

The product life cycle represents the consumer's view of the product. The product life cycle consists of the major stages that a product will progress through during the product's life span. The product life cycle, as depicted in Figure 4.2, consists of the following four stages for an innovative product that is dominant:

- **Dominant product:** The product creates a new market.

- **Feature set expansion:** Features are added that improve the consumer experience.

- **Feature overkill:** Features are added beyond consumer need.

- **Commoditized product:** Competition commoditizes the product.

As we will see, not all products will progress through all four stages of the product life cycle. Introducing a new disruptive innovation can destroy an existing dominant product's market long before the dominant product reaches commoditization. Conversely, products that are unique may exist in a monopoly state and never progress to commoditization.

Figure 4.2 provides a graphical depiction of the product life cycle.

Stage 1: Dominant Product

When a product is introduced to the market, it could arrive as the dominant product, or it may have to rise to the level of market dominance by displacing existing product offerings. Thus, the dominant product stage could be any length of time from very short to extremely long.

An example of a product that arrived as the dominant product is the Apple iPhone. Since the iPhone largely created the smartphone market, it was

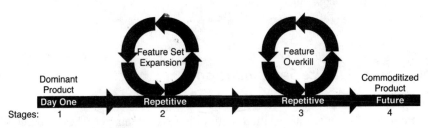

FIGURE 4.2 Product life cycle

instantly perceived by many as the dominant product within that market. (With all due respect to RIM, which pioneered the first handheld phone that provided corporate email support, the iPhone was the first true smartphone.)

A product that does not become the dominant product in the market will start in stage 2 of the product life cycle. This is because the company will begin to aggressively enhance the product through feature set expansion.

Conversely, a product with little or no competitive pressures may remain in stage 1 of the product life cycle for many years. This is generally the stage that a product with a monopoly market position will remain in. The deregulation of certain industries, such as power and communications, are examples of attempts to force products into stage 2 of the product life cycle by removing the existing product offering from a position of dominance within the market.

In some cases, companies bring new products to market knowing that they cannot achieve immediate market dominance. In these cases, it is critical that the new entrants immediately progress to stage 2 of the product life cycle. Otherwise, the existing dominant product will begin to be enhanced, and the new product will likely remain in a continuous position of trying to catch up to the dominant incumbent product.

A dominant product that remains in stage 1 of the product life cycle will, over time, increase the risk of being displaced by new product entrants. New products based on a new disruptive innovation, as well as new products with expanded features, can quickly enter the market and become dominant.

BOB SHOULD CONSIDER

- Are our products stuck in stage 1 of the product life cycle? If so, is this optimal?
- Do we need to accelerate our product life cycle in order to create a dominant product?
- Should we delay deployment and increase the baseline features of our product in order to force our competition into a trailing position with us within the product life cycle?

Stage 2: Feature Set Expansion

In stage 2 of the product life cycle, an existing product is enhanced in ways to improve or maintain its position within the existing market. These enhancements could be new features or changes in marketing. For the sake of this discussion, marketing shifts are covered in the market life cycle discussed later.

A product evolves naturally into stage 2 of the product life cycle for several reasons:

- The product has failed to achieve market dominance in its original form.
- Competition is challenging the product's current market dominance.
- The consumer's transformative value of the product is changing.
- The company has identified untapped or poorly tapped markets for the product that require new features to penetrate.
- The company has chosen to enter the market with an interim version and immediately scale up the feature set to exceed the feature set of the existing dominant product.

In stage 2 of the product life cycle, new features added to the product are those perceived to have a positive transformative value to the consumer. During stage 2, asking the consumer "What do you want?" can deliver positive results. The consumer can identify shortcomings in the existing product offerings, even if the product is currently dominant, and can assist the company in expanding the features of the product. As we will discuss in stage 3 of the product life cycle, there comes a point when it becomes potentially dangerous to rely on consumer feedback for product evolution.

Figure 4.3 depicts the pressures that will move a product from stage 1 of the product life cycle into stage 2, and the figure also depicts the pressures that can keep a product stable in stage 1. Note that the pressures that keep a

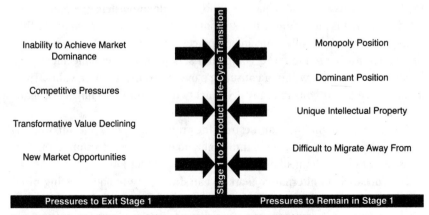

Figure 4.3 Product life cycle stages 1 and 2 transition pressures

product in stage 1 imply continued market dominance even if they are not perceived positively by the consumer. But, the entry of new competitive pressures can quickly cancel out these "stay in stage 1" pressures and immediately drive a product to stage 2. Unfortunately, when a product is forced into stage 2, the product will often be behind other competitive products relative to distinguishing features that can reacquire market dominance.

All of the reasons listed previously for entering stage 2 of the product life cycle are critical to consider and understand. But, the one that is most often overlooked is when a change in the consumer's transformative value for the product has occurred.

The transformative value for a product can decrease because of many types of changes, including the following:

- Shifts within consumer buying preferences

- Introduction of new product features within competing products

- Disruptive innovations that have shifted a consumer's demand for your product to a completely different product

- New products that have been introduced in alternative markets and that have shifted certain feature requirements out of your product's market

- Economic shifts that cause your product to either exceed or fall below the concept of a "good enough" product

Shifts within consumer buying preferences can continuously reset the transformative value of all products within the impacted market. Clothing styles are a perfect example. Seasonal shifts can cause consumer preferences to change relative to colors, patterns, cloth texture, and density.

Enhancements to a competitor's products can do far more damage than simply shifting some of a consumer's perceived value of your product onto the competitor's product. The competitor's new feature enhancements can create new dynamics within a consumer's overall transformative value. These dynamics can shift consumer loyalty quickly and nullify the impact of many of your product's existing features.

Disruptive innovations can destroy the transformative value for existing products by shifting consumers into a new market. These disruptive innovations are often not immediately recognized as product killers.

New products in alternative markets can drastically impact existing products. For instance, the introduction of higher-density disc drives at lower costs for personal computers created a new storage medium for music. Over several years, multidisc CD players began to vanish from the stereo receiver market because of the disc drive product improvements within the computer industry. Continued feature enhancement to the multidisc CD players no longer had any positive impact on the consumer's transformative value.

In some cases, changes in the transformative value can be corrected by new feature expansion. In other cases, it is impossible to increase the transformative value through feature expansion. This makes it critical that the company recognize the need to restart the product life cycle with new product offerings. We will discuss later some specific approaches that can be used to maintain and even increase the transformative value of your product and how to ensure that expanded features continue to deliver value to the consumer.

If a product is in a competitive market, continuous feature expansion will eventually drive the product from stage 2 to stage 3 of the product life cycle.

BOB SHOULD CONSIDER

- Why did our product enter stage 2 of the product life cycle?
- When considering what features to add to our product, are we fully considering all of the external pressures on our product?
- Has the transformative value of our product changed? Why?
- How should we respond to a change in the transformative value of our product?
- Are we properly positioning our feature enhancements to minimize our risks?

Stage 3: Feature Overkill

We discussed in Chapter 3 the concept of negative incremental inventions. From a product life cycle point of view, this is referred to as **feature overkill**.

In an informal poll of innovation consultants, I found that about 80% of innovation consultants will recommend that you involve your customer in your product evolution and in your search for new disruptive innovations. These consultants will say things similar to "No one knows better what they need than the actual customer."

It is important to understand that once a product has moved from stage 2 to stage 3 of the product life cycle, there is probably little value in attempting to continue to utilize the average consumer as a "What do you want/need?"

sounding board. This is not because of a lack of skill on the part of the consumer. It is just that the existing products have reached the point that incremental invention probably no longer delivers positive transformative value changes. Once the product has reached the "good enough" point, it is very difficult for the consumer to visualize an alternative product offering.

Once a product enters stage 3 of the product life cycle, continuing to deliver new product feature enhancements will result in many negative changes:

- The product complexity increases.

- Product stability will generally decrease.

- The transformative value begins to fall and begins to equalize across competitors.

- Customer loyalty to particular products may vanish completely as transformative value for all competing products equalizes.

- Prices start to fall, and margins start to shrink.

- Additional competitive products with similar features will enter the market.

- The probability of a disruptive innovation causing a product shift increases dramatically.

These changes work together within stage 3 of the product life cycle to accelerate the product toward commoditization.

Products within stage 3 have most likely reached the definition of a "good enough" product described in Chapter 1. This "good enough" threshold makes it inherently simpler for new, highly competitive products to arise that have a lower product cost and yet deliver a similar transformative value.

Figure 4.4 shows how the transformative value for the dominant product and competing products will both continue to rise until the dominant product enters stage 3 of the product life cycle. This transition point between stages 2 and 3 of the product life cycle is depicted as product inflection point B. Similarly, the transition point between stages 3 and 4 of the product life cycle is depicted as product inflection point C. These inflection points will be discussed in detail shortly. For the purposes of alignment with the innovation life cycle, there is no product inflection point A.

Companies have several options of how to avoid remaining in stage 3, feature overkill, and how to avoid progressing to stage 4, commoditization, of the product life cycle. These will be discussed in detail later in the book.

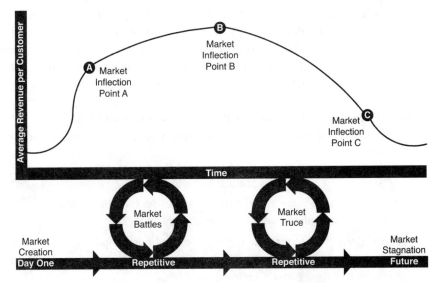

FIGURE 4.9   Average revenue per customer

Stage 1: Market Creation

A new market is created when a disruptive innovation is created. Since the introductory, dominant product that "founded" the market is based on a disruptive innovation, it is unlikely that there is a large amount of competition already in place. It will likely take some time, be it anywhere from weeks to years, for competitive products to be delivered with sufficient features to compete effectively against the dominant product.

In the market creation stage of the market life cycle, customer churn for the dominant product is relatively flat since there is little competition within the market. As depicted in Figure 4.8 at inflection point A, more and more competitors are entering the market, and the rate of churn begins to rise. It is too early to tell at inflection point A if the dominant product is losing its position within the market. As discussed earlier, inflection point A on the innovation life cycle is also the point at which the dominant company begins incremental innovation in earnest and disruptive innovation aftershocks could still be occurring. If the dominant company is successful in maintaining a low churn rate, then the market life cycle will appear to hang between inflection points A and B.

During the early part of the market creation stage, the ARPC will probably appear to be relatively flat. This is because of the initial start-up costs and expansion of infrastructure costs. Once this period is past, increased production will lower per-product costs. Since competitors are still developing and positioning their products, the ARPC could appear to rise dramatically prior to inflection point A. The rate of increase in the ARPC may not dip until inflection point A is reached, when competitors aggressively start to enter the market.

We will discuss in detail in Part III why it is important at this stage for competitive companies to attempt to dramatically increase customer churn.

BOB SHOULD CONSIDER

- If our market is in stage 1 of the market life cycle, is customer churn high or low? How do we utilize this to our advantage?
- Are we attempting to increase the churn rate of our competitor's dominant product? Are we utilizing new features to accomplish this or lowering our price and decreasing our ARPC?
- How can we minimize our churn rate and maximize our competitor's churn rate?
- How can we maximize our ARPC and minimize our competitor's ARPC?

Stage 2: Market Battles

In stage 2 of the market life cycle, most competitors will be aggressively modifying and enhancing their products in order to maintain or obtain the dominant market position.

When more competitors enter the market, they can dramatically accelerate the market life cycle to the detriment of all companies.

One of the major risks in stage 2 is that your company's product enhancements will be duplicated and expanded on by the dominant company. This will have the following impacts:

- **It will nullify any shift in transformative value:** The transformative value for the market overall may increase, but your product's transformative value will remain stable relative to the transformative value of the dominant product.

- **It will maintain or even lower the customer churn rate for the dominant company:** It is critical that new feature enhancements deliver an increase in your competitor's customer churn.

not intended to be all-encompassing. They are merely defined to impart the primary drivers of decision makers when it comes to making decisions relative to the innovation life cycle:

- **Revenue expectations:** Demands for making money

- **Customer commitments:** Making money

- **Vested interests:** Utilizing already spent money

Note that all three categories of pressures revolve around money. That is because business decision makers, at least good business decision makers, consider money before they consider technology. A product that is amazing to a technologist will only be amazing to a businessperson if the product can actually make money.

Figure 4-12 depicts how these pressures can drastically reduce the flexibility that management teams have when it comes to making decisions.

One of the side effects of reducing decision-making options is that the management team must improve in quality to counterbalance the loss of decision-making flexibility. A so-so manager can perform well when the pressures are low and there is a great deal of flexibility about what is the "best" decision. That same manager will likely fail when the flexibility vanishes and making the wrong decision is a matter of company survival.

This is one reason that a highly successful start-up that is run by technologists can eventually face serious problems and the company can fail. The

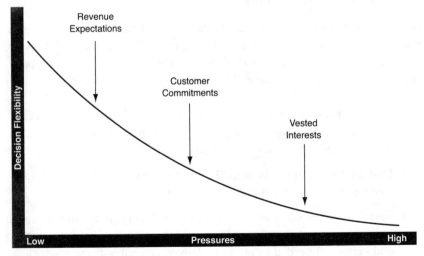

FIGURE 4.12 Decision flexibility

technology executive didn't lose any skills. But, the decision-making process has completely changed.

Here are some of the ways that can be used to reduce the pressures:

- **Revenue expectation:** Find new investors to replace the old ones. Buy back stock. Pay off or renegotiate debt.

- **Customer commitments:** Decline large product commitments for customers who have a low return on investment. In some cases, large customers can be a seriously limiting burden.

- **Vested interests:** Consolidate infrastructure, lay off or move personnel, outsource, and modernize.

BOB SHOULD CONSIDER

- What are the pressures that impact our ability to make decisions?
- If these pressures did not exist, would we make the same product innovation decisions that we are currently making?
- Are the decisions we are making relative to our product innovation being impacted by the actions of our competition? Would we make the same decisions if we ignored our competition?

Stage 1: Initial Flexibility

When a company enters a new market, the executives and management teams within the company will generally have a great deal of flexibility relative to the products within that new market. Some of the reasons that the pressures on decision-making flexibility will be low include the following:

- **Revenue expectations:** The company most likely entered the market with an understanding that revenues would increase over time. Initial revenue expectations should be reasonable.

- **Customer commitments:** Initially the company will have few, if any, customers demanding specific new features.

- **Vested interests:** Compared to companies with large, established customer bases, the stage 1 company has very little invested in infrastructures and personnel needed to produce, deliver, and support the product.

This initial flexibility allows the innovation life cycle to proceed optimally through its first initial stages as well. But, as we discussed in Chapter 3, deceleration of growth at innovation inflection point A will likely force the management team to begin moving down an aggressive incremental innovation path.

It is in stage 1 of the company life cycle that a company will normally begin spending larger and larger sums building out the vested interests required to sell, deliver, and support the product. Sales success will immediately begin to increase pressures on decision-making flexibility in all three categories.

One of the greatest risks throughout the company life cycle, especially in stage 1 of the company life cycle, is that the management team will enter a push-me/pull-you model with the competitors. In this model, multiple things begin to happen:

1. **Pull-you action**: Companies deliver new features to attract uncommitted customers.

2. **Push-me reaction**: Competitors match these new features to attract the same uncommitted customers.

3. **Pull-you action**: Companies deliver new features in response to specific requests from existing customers.

4. **Push-me reaction**: Competitors match these new features in order to try to steal these customers.

5. **Pull-you action**: Large potential customers issue requests for proposals (RFPs) that lay out numerous features that they want to see in a product.

6. **Push-me reaction**: All competitors attempt to deliver the features in order to win the large customer.

The impact of the push-me/pull-you model is that the product direction is basically no longer controlled by the company. The push-me/pull-you model has shifted control of product direction into the hands of the market and out of the hands of product development.

This push-me/pull-you model has many effects on the company. Some of these effects include the following:

- **Accelerated feature delivery**: To remain "competitive," new push-me reaction features are often delivered without any time to determine the success within the market of those same features delivered by the pull-you competitor.

- **Product road map:** The feature content within the product road map quickly becomes based on push-me reactions and not long-term planning.

- **Product architecture:** Because of the knee-jerk reaction inherent in the push-me/pull-you model, the architecture of the product quickly becomes suboptimal and continues to deteriorate.

- **Support infrastructure:** As push-me reaction features are delivered, the internal support structure must be expanded and modified quickly to handle these new features.

In essence, the features delivered in a push-me reaction begin to drive the products and the market. But, the internal impacts of the push-me/pull-you model can be catastrophic over time. The first company to deliver a new feature (a pull-you action) will likely deliver it with the least negative internal company impact: best road map, best architecture, best infrastructure. All competing companies that respond (a push-me reaction) with a competitive feature will likely deliver the feature in a suboptimal manner: disrupted road map, suboptimal architecture, inefficient infrastructure. Over time, the push-me/pull-you model will deliver negative inventions to the market, create extremely complicated product architectures, and create an internal infrastructure with large numbers of inefficiencies. Each time a company responds within the push-me/pull-you model, the costs, commitments, and complexities of future feature deliveries will likely increase.

The one good aspect of the push-me/pull-you model, if it can be called good, is that the push-me/pull-you model is equally damaging to all competitors. One company will be in the pull-you action role and then will swap places and be in the push-me reaction role. This back and forth exchange of the push-me and pull-you roles will probably degrade all companies within the market. As more competitors enter the market, the push-me/pull-you model will likely accelerate and become even more damaging.

Figure 4.13 depicts the push-me/pull-you model.

BOB SHOULD CONSIDER

- Are we taking advantage of the fact that our company pressures are currently low?

- Are we trapped in a push-me/pull-you feature delivery model?

- How can we avoid the push-me/pull-you model and compete effectively?

- Is there a way that we can use the push-me/pull-you model to our advantage within the market? Can we control the model?

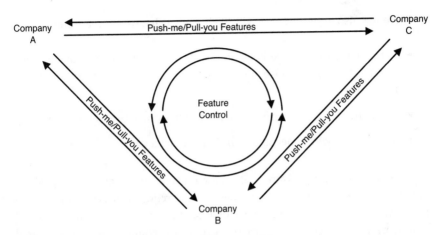

FIGURE 4.13 Push-me/pull-you feature delivery model

Stage 2: Pressures

In stage 2 of the company life cycle, pressures are continuing to build on the management team, and decision-making flexibility is decreasing. Even if the company has been very successful in stage 1 and has avoided increasing revenue pressures, that very success has probably increased the customer commitment and vested interests pressures.

Unless a company is doing a superb job of balancing these pressures, the following are some trends that are probably occurring in stage 2 of the company life cycle:

- The push-me/pull-you model is dominating new feature definition.

- Incremental innovations are largely derived from pull-you reactions.

- Innovations are shifting from external to internal to support increased vested interest requirements.

- The product is approaching and passing the "good enough" state for the majority of the consumers.

- The product complexity is increasing.

- Building a "good enough" product from the existing product is becoming more difficult.

- Smaller customers are being abandoned in order to pursue higher-revenue customers.

There are also activities that will likely be accelerating these trends:

- The delivery of negative inventions will increasingly force management to rely more on the push-me/pull-you feature model for new innovations.

- The entrance of new competitors is driving down prices and revenues.

- Revenue growth is becoming difficult to achieve.

In short, company pressures will likely escalate to the point that positive incremental innovation ceases and negative incremental invention predominates. These company pressures will force the innovation life cycle to proceed into its negative, later stages. Once this occurs, the company is headed toward stage 3 of the company life cycle. Executive management must fully understand how to restart the innovation life cycle and be willing to make decisions with the goal of restarting innovation in mind. In Part III we will discuss how to restart the innovation life cycle.

It is critical that management disrupts the company life cycle before entering stage 3.

BOB SHOULD CONSIDER

- Are we still delivering positive incremental innovations, or have we begun to deliver negative incremental inventions?
- Can we balance capital expenditures and align them with the innovation life cycle so as to minimize the growth of company pressures?
- Can our competitors use our company pressures against us? How can we defend against this?
- Are our executive mandates forcing our product groups to respond first to the push-me/pull-you model? How can we fix this?
- What stage of the company life cycle are our competitors in? Can we use this to our advantage?

Stage 3: Frozen Flexibility

Once a company enters stage 3 of the company life cycle, it is very difficult, though not impossible, to restart the innovation life cycle and by inference restart the company life cycle. Unfortunately, many companies find that they must take drastic action in order to reduce the company pressures and increase decision-making flexibility. Often, the first decision is to slash costs no matter what is required. A mandate such as "layoff 15% of all employees in each department" is an excellent example. Although some of the wrong people may be laid off, in general company operating costs will be slashed, and decision-making flexibility will increase.

Each new decision, if properly decided and then implemented, will further increase the decision-making flexibility. However, it is critical that the management team remember that the goal is to restart the innovation life cycle. Unless the company can create a disruptive innovation and shift to a new company life cycle, the lowering of company pressures through difficult actions will deliver only temporary benefits.

The Company Life Cycle and the Innovation Life Cycle

Figure 4.14 shows how the innovation life cycle and the company life cycle align. It is important to remember that the innovation life cycle is from the view of the product development team and that the company life cycle is from the view of the management team.

Since the management team has a direct impact on the decision-making flexibility of the product development team, the company life cycle and innovation life cycle are highly interwoven, and in most cases the company life

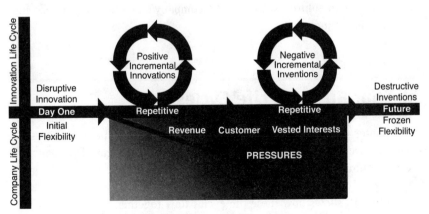

FIGURE 4.14 Company life cycle and innovation life cycle

cycle will win out. So, as depicted in Figure 4-14, unlike the other business life cycles, the company life cycle causes the stages of the innovation life cycle:

- Initial flexibility extends the disruptive innovation aftershocks.

- Increasing company pressures shift the innovation life cycle from positive incremental innovations to negative incremental inventions.

- Frozen flexibility greatly limits decision-making options and increases pressure to deliver inventions even if they become destructive inventions.

You may have noticed that we did not discuss inflection points during our review of the company life cycle. This was not an oversight. There are multiple views from within the company life cycle, and each has a different approach to maximizing the value of the innovation life cycle. These different views will be discussed in detail in the chapters within Part III and consist of the following:

- **Innovating from scratch:** Finding a new invention and innovation

- **IT solution innovation:** Innovating internally

- **Innovating to dominate:** Remaining dominant in the market

- **Innovating to conquer:** Becoming dominant in the market

- **Innovating to disrupt:** Creating new disruptive innovations from an existing market

- **Products to solutions:** Evolving a company's product innovations into solutions innovations

All Four Business Life Cycles

This chapter has described the product, market, and company business life cycles. As we have seen, these life cycles have a great deal of influence on the innovation life cycle. Conversely, the innovation life cycle can have a huge impact on the other business life cycles.

Figure 4.15 shows how these life cycles flow together.

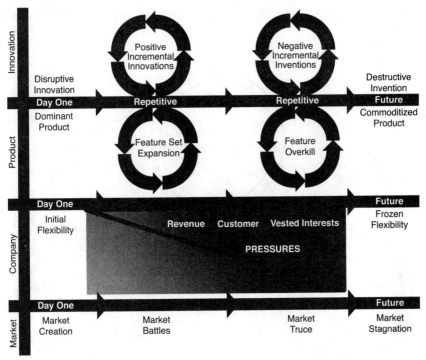

FIGURE 4.15 The business life cycles

The following summarizes what we have discussed concerning these impacts:

- Disruptive innovations will create a dominant product and create a new market. The duration of disruptive innovation aftershocks are extended by a company's initial flexibility.

- Positive incremental innovations deliver new features and allow the company to wage market battles with competitors. Company pressures can stop positive incremental innovation.

- Negative incremental inventions create feature overkill and indicate that market battles should end, and a market truce should be declared. Company pressures can increase the tendency to deliver negative incremental inventions.

- Destructive inventions contribute to product commoditization and market stagnation. Frozen flexibility increases pressure to deliver inventions even if they are destructive inventions.

Figure 4.16 depicts the impacts between the life cycles described in the previous list.

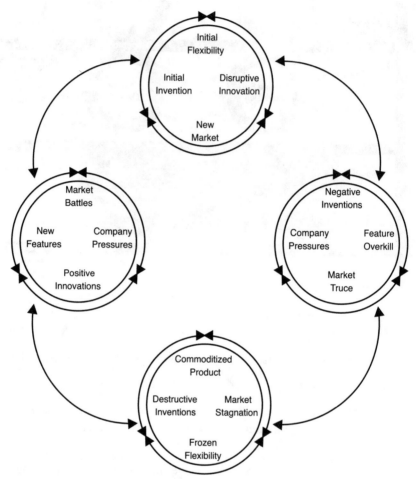

FIGURE 4.16 Business life cycle impacts

5

Innovation Life Cycle Stagnation

In Chapter 2 we looked at the transformative value of a product from the consumer's viewpoint and how critical it is to maximize that transformative value. In Chapter 3 we discussed the innovation life cycle and how there are points within the life cycle that create an appearance of randomness within the innovation process. Chapter 4, through the introduction of the company life cycle, the market life cycle, and the product life cycle, demonstrated that there are multiple views of the same processes that are occurring throughout the innovation life cycle.

In this chapter, we will introduce the transformative value chain and demonstrate that a product has a transformative value to all the stakeholders in the product delivery chain including the consumer. We will examine why positive innovation almost always seems to stagnate, forcing the innovation life cycle to run to its ultimate, negative conclusions.

Innovation Life Cycle Pressures

The innovation life cycle as described in Chapter 3 demonstrates how the innovation life cycle functions within virtually all company environments. The innovation life cycle ultimately ends when further innovation is counterproductive and lowers the transformative value of the product. There must be pressures that are driving the life cycle that are either difficult to identify or difficult to control or both.

There are likely many ways to summarize the pressures that drive the innovation life cycle. For the purposes of this book, I have summarized these pressures into three primary questions:

- Why do executives view innovation as a risk?

- Why do management teams have difficulty with the next innovation?

- Why do competitors seem to have an advantage within the latter stages of the innovation life cycle?

The answers to each of these questions, to varying degrees, are impacted by three areas that we will cover in some depth in this chapter:

- Appearance of randomness

- Overlapping viewpoints

- Product commoditization

Appearance of Randomness

While we were discussing the innovation life cycle in Chapter 3, we touched briefly on some of the key points within the life cycle at which randomness appeared to enter the perception of the process of product innovation. These key points from Chapter 3 can be summarized as follows:

- Extrapolation of need from a sample to the entire potential market

- Incomplete definition of the transformative value

- Invalid definition of the market's needs for the product

- Inability to project product success

- Inability to predict whether a product will be disruptive or merely competitive

- Disruptive innovation spikes through poor consumer perception of the product

What is counterintuitive is that all of these points of randomness are related to a single, multitiered relationship: the relationship of the product to the consumer and the relationship of the consumer to the market.

A venture capital–funded start-up that had spent more than $40 million to date recently asked me, "Where can we sell our product?" During the development of its product, the market had shifted, and the consumer's transformative value for the product had plummeted. By the time the product was ready, the market had vanished. The start-up may have started with a faulty understanding of the transformative value, or it may have failed to monitor the transformative value during product development.

Rephrasing and combining these points of randomness, we arrive at the following requirements that should be fulfilled prior to product development and deployment:

- Detailed determination and analysis of the markets for the product

- Definition of the transformative value for each consumer subgroup

- Optimal mapping and marketing of product features to each consumer's transformative value

- Definition of a "good enough" product that will meet the needs of the consumers

Exceeding what constitutes a "good enough" product on an initial product development and introduction will likely expend funds and time on a product that may not require functionality beyond "good enough" in order to dominate the market. Quite often time to market is a critical competitive factor. This increased cost can ultimately translate into a longer return on investment cycle. In addition, the increased complexity for the consumer to utilize additional features beyond "good enough" can result in a decrease in the consumer's transformative value for the product and shrink the potential consumer market size. These negative impacts brought on by delivering a seemingly better initial product will increase the appearance of randomness in new product innovation.

As we mentioned briefly in Chapter 2, the incorrect mapping of product features to the consumer's transformative value can improperly increase the consumer's initial perceived transformative value for the product, causing a disruptive innovation spike. These spikes drive up the initial success of the product only to have the sales plummet shortly after product introduction. The causes of such spikes are very hard to identify without a complete reevaluation of the market, of the consumer's transformative value, and of the product features as well as the marketing efforts. The apparent unexplainable nature of product sales spikes can contribute greatly to the perception of randomness within innovation.

Each consumer subgroup within the targeted markets can have a slightly, or even drastically, different transformative value. The lifestyle impacts for the product within these subgroups can vary greatly. Taking a broad view of these subgroups and treating them as one whole market will probably incorrectly attribute lifestyle impacts to all of the consumer subgroups driving product development beyond the level of "good enough" for the majority of the consumers. Introducing a product to a particular consumer subgroup that exceeds a "good enough" level can keep the transformative value within that subgroup low. Thus, incorrectly blending consumer subgroups will randomize the lifestyle impacts and make it very difficult to isolate consumer needs in order to increase the product's transformative value.

When determining market size, we will often hear statements like "All people who own an . . ." or "All existing users of . . . ." These categorizations of consumers and markets can greatly expand the definition of the potential market size of a new product. In reality, the consumers within these larger existing markets ("All people who own an . . .") actually exist within many subgroups that have drastically different transformative values with different lifestyle impacts. The worst possible outcome of this market-level assumption of a consistent consumer is seen when the majority of the existing consumers have already purchased a product that has reached or exceeded a "good enough" level. These consumers may be very difficult to shift to a new product or market. This overexpansion of the potential market will likely result in product sales below initial projection and can create a perceived randomness within the innovation of a new product.

Figure 5.1 depicts how these four requirements that must be fulfilled prior to product development and deployment should be integrated and maintained in order to maximize the potential success of a product. It is not sufficient to just initially define each of these requirements. As the figure depicts, the requirements must be continuously reevaluated in order to properly reflect changes in markets, transformative values, feature mapping, and the definition of a "good enough" product.

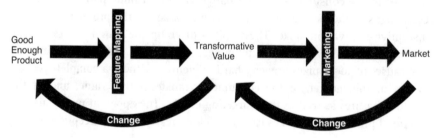

FIGURE 5.1 Impact of market changes on products

BOB SHOULD CONSIDER

- Are we attempting to deliver an initial product that exceeds a "good enough" product?
- Have we assumed that the transformative value of all consumers within our target market(s) is the same?
- Are we properly monitoring our target market and our potential consumers to understand and react to any changes?
- Are our marketing materials designed to optimally reflect our products benefits relative to our consumers' transformative value and to maximize our product's lifestyle impact?

Overlapping Viewpoints

As we discussed in Chapter 4, there are many potential viewpoints of what is occurring during the progression of the innovation life cycle. We summarized these as the market life cycle, the product life cycle, and the company life cycle. These and other viewpoints are always overlapping in the minds of management teams and product developers.

Without a method to isolate these viewpoints, discussions on how to properly enhance a product often result in the team "talking in circles" where each group constantly tries to draw attention back to its area of the product delivery chain. This only makes sense because each group is a specialist in a particular area. The product developers are not marketing people. The marketing people are not manufacturers.

The apparent inability to define successful, disruptive innovations within a product space will often toggle ownership of a product between the product development group and the marketing group. Each will be given the opportunity to define the next set of features for the product road map.

As we will see shortly, the "talking in circles" problem does not need to exist. There is a simple approach that will allow targeting of innovation to deliver successful product features to the market.

As depicted in Figure 4.16 in Chapter 4, the "talking in circles" problem can become extremely difficult to eliminate since it can become so pervasive within the company and because each view can be in different stages.

> ### BOB SHOULD CONSIDER
> - Are our teams talking in circles?
> - Who should manage the definition of future product features?

Product Commoditization

In Chapter 2 we discussed the concept of a product's transformative value and how that transformative value can vary from one consumer to another. To better understand how a product and market become commoditized, we will expand the concept of transformative value.

A consumer will have a transformative value that is a reflection of that consumer's willingness to purchase a particular product. Conversely, from the product manufacturer's point of view, this relationship can be summarized as the "revenue value" of the product to the company. For each company/product/consumer relationship, there will be both a transformative value and a revenue value. Figure 5.2 depicts this relationship.

The transformative value/revenue value relationship appears straightforward at first. But, the relationship is far more complex than a simple input/output-type relationship. In most cases, the transformative value will decrease over time because of many of the factors discussed in earlier chapters including competition, negative incremental invention, and destructive invention. This natural tendency for the transformative value to decrease, regardless of the actions of the company, creates a huge amount of stress between the transformative value and the revenue value.

Companies following the innovation life cycle (or the product life cycle more likely) will continue to deliver features to an existing product in order to increase the transformative value of the product. The company expects a corresponding increase in the revenue value to occur concurrently.

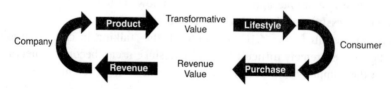

FIGURE 5.2 Transformative value and revenue value

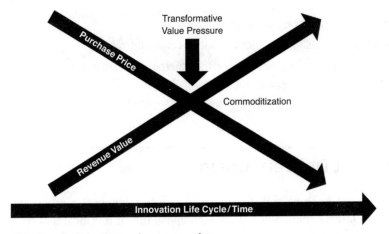

FIGURE 5.3 Commoditization and revenue value

A company's perceived revenue value will create the perception, and often the reality, of product commoditization. Figure 5.3 depicts a general view of the inverse flows of these two values and when commoditization arises within the market. When the transformative value will no longer support the price of the product needed to meet the companies desired revenue value, the market is most likely headed toward commoditization.

Oftentimes a company will spin off a product line into a new company in an effort to realign the transformative value of the product with the corresponding revenue value of the product. Reducing product delivery costs will likely decrease the required revenue value and result in a new competitive positioning within the market. As we will see in the next chapter, there are other ways to realign these two values.

It should be noted that unless a new disruptive innovation is delivered that shifts the consumer into a new market, it is likely that a consumer will still perceive the product as a component of their lifestyle with a positive transformative value. This can remain true, even if the commoditization situation depicted in Figure 5.3 has occurred. It is this inherent survivability of the positive transformative value of a product that gives companies the opportunity to reinnovate within an existing market.

Bob Should Consider

- Has our product's transformative value fallen?
- Are we repeatedly increasing our projected revenue value requirements?

continues

- Has our product entered commoditization?
- How can we shift our product out of commoditization?
- How can we take advantage of the inherent survivability of the positive transformative value of our product?

Product Delivery Chain

Later in this book we will demonstrate how to reinnovate a product/market that has largely commoditized. To accomplish this, it is critical that we define a structure of how products are produced and delivered to the final consumer. We will call this the **product delivery chain**. The product delivery chain consists of one or more stakeholders (companies) who are involved in the development and sales of the particular product.

The product delivery chain can be very short or extremely long and complex. For our purposes, we will designate the following stakeholders within the product delivery chain:

- **Supplier:** One or more companies that provide components of the final product

- **Manufacturer:** One or more companies that assemble or manufacture the final product

- **Distributor:** One or more companies that act as a distributor of the final manufactured product

- **Value-added reseller (VAR):** One or more companies that enhance the final product in some way to enhance the targeting of particular consumer subgroups

- **Installer:** One or more companies that deliver, install, support, or otherwise act as the "front line" for the product

- **Consumer:** One or more consumer subgroups that have a positive transformative value for the product and consume the product in some way

Figure 5.4 shows how these product delivery chain stakeholders interrelate relative to the product. Obviously, these functional stakeholders are intended to be representative and not definitive. Your product may involve more or

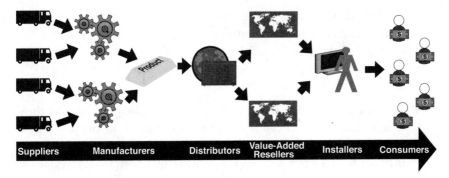

| Suppliers | Manufacturers | Distributors | Value-Added Resellers | Installers | Consumers |

FIGURE 5.4 Product delivery chain

fewer stakeholders. In addition, some or all of the functions may occur in-house within your company while others occur externally.

During our discussions of these stakeholders, it is important to understand how they can be applied to multiple industries. For instance, let's assume that we are a pharmaceutical company and that our product is a drug delivery system with a pump-like device. In this sample scenario, our six stakeholders would likely take on the following functions:

- **Supplier:** Components such as electronics, tubing, software, raw drug materials

- **Manufacturer:** Pump, packaging, storage box, drug manufacturing

- **Distributor:** Payee, insurer, government agency

- **Value-added reseller:** Doctor, physician, hospital

- **Installer:** Primary caregiver, nurse, in-home care, loved one

- **Consumer:** Patient

Even if many of these functions are occurring internally within your company, it is still wise to view them as separate stakeholders within the product delivery chain. You should define your product delivery chain to include as many stakeholders needed in order to reflect potential risks to production, risks to sales, and risks to transformative value. The previous pharmaceutical case can be summarized as follows to reflect these risks:

- **Production risks:** Production risks can include areas such as the supplier being unable to deliver or the manufacturer owning all the intellectual property of the drug delivery product.

- **Sales risks:** Sales risks can include a lack of approval from government agencies or an unwillingness of insurance companies to cover the costs of the treatment. Sales risks can also include an unwillingness of doctors to prescribe the treatment because of a poor understanding or balance of risk to cost and benefit.

- **Transformative value risks:** Risks to the transformative value of the drug delivery product can come from the caregivers or the patients. Because the proper management of such a treatment regimen often includes both a caregiver and the patient, the transformative value of the product is controlled and defined by both.

The management of the relationship with each of the shareholders within the product delivery chain is critical to the ongoing success of the product and the ability to innovate new products.

BOB SHOULD CONSIDER

- Who are the stakeholders in our product delivery chain?
- Where in our product delivery chain are our risks of impacting production, sales, and transformative value?
- Do we have both external and internal stakeholders?

Transformative Value Chain

Up until this point, we have discussed the concept of transformative value as if it applies specifically to an individual consumer of a product. In reality, the principle of transformative value can be used to analyze and value any relationship that involves the exchange of one resource (for example, money) for another resource (for example, product).

Each of the stakeholders in the product delivery chain represents a separate application of the transformative value/revenue value relationship. For instance, a supplier sells your company a particular component. That component has a transformative value to your company, and the cost of the component has a specific revenue value to the supplier.

Figure 5.5 demonstrates how the product delivery chain consists of multiple transformative value/revenue value relationships. It is important to note

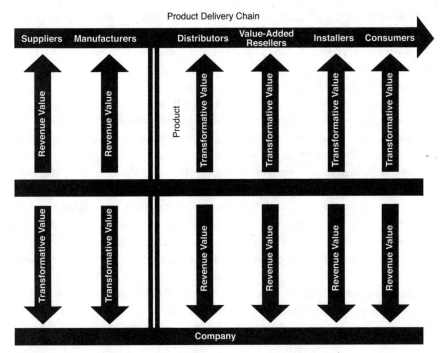

FIGURE 5.5 Transformative value chain

that, in general, the transformative value is internal to the company prior to the completion of the product and then becomes external to the company after completing the manufacturing of the product. In Figure 5.5, to the left of the product line, the suppliers and manufacturers constitute the product supply chain. They are driven by revenues, and the company is driven by the transformative value of the components being purchased from the suppliers and manufacturers. After the product is constructed, to the right of the product line in Figure 5.5, the roles shift from supply to distribution. Each of the players on the distribution side is now driven by the transformative value of the product, and the company is driven by revenues.

Just as in the case of an individual consumer, each of the transformative value/revenue value relationships will be defined by many aspects such as quality, suitability, flexibility, and other areas that impact the business lifestyle of the company. The most flexible aspect will probably be cost (assuming that the cost of production and the price of consumption remain consistent with each other as costs rise and fall). In other words, decreasing the cost of a product will likely increase the transformative value and decrease the revenue value. Therefore, in this case, cost would have an inverse impact on the two values.

If the company can reduce cost of production without lowering the price of consumption, then the transformative value would remain the same while the revenue value would rise. This is the situation that most companies hope for but find difficult or impossible to sustain for long periods of time because of increased competition.

The transformative value chain depicted in Figure 5.5 can become even more complex when we view the relationships between the stakeholders following the final production of the product: distributors, value-added resellers, installers, and consumers. These stakeholders probably function serially within guidelines defined by the company. Therefore, these stakeholders have their own transformative value/revenue value relationships, as depicted in Figure 5.6.

Figure 5.6 may appear to be transformative value/revenue value overkill. The intent is to demonstrate how a change in the transformative value or the revenue value for any stakeholders within any relationship within the transformative value chain can cause a tectonic shift through the entire transformative value chain.

This tectonic shift occurs because each stakeholder will adjust as needed in an attempt to reflect the change either in the transformative value or in the revenue value. Most often, these types of shifts are mitigated through additional positive incremental innovation of the product. Although shifts in the transformative value chain may translate into increased prices, the additional positive incremental innovations balance out the impacts of these price increases on the consumer's transformative value for the product. Unless there is room for positive incremental innovations that can justify a price of consumption increase, the following will likely occur:

- One or more stakeholders, including the consumer, will have to absorb the price increase.

- The transformative value of the product for all stakeholders will fall.

- The revenue value of all stakeholders must increase to absorb the price increase.

- Cost cutting will likely commence within the various stakeholders in order to realign the price or to stabilize the transformative value.

- Incremental invention will accelerate to justify the price increase.

- The probability of entering negative incremental invention or destructive invention will increase.

Essentially, any price increase will decrease transformative value, increase cost cutting, and accelerate the innovation life cycle.

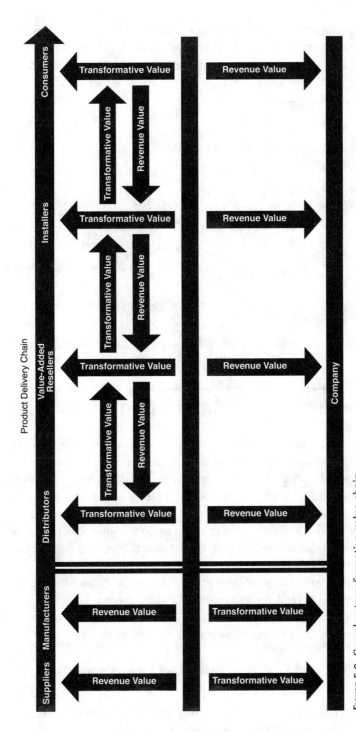

FIGURE 5.6 Complex transformative value chain

As the number of stakeholders in a product delivery chain increases, the ability to understand why product sales are increasing or decreasing becomes more difficult to quantify. As we will see in Chapter 6, to control the transformative value chain and the innovation life cycle, we must monitor and respond accordingly to each of the stakeholders.

BOB SHOULD CONSIDER

- What is our transformative value chain?
- Are there internal relationships between our stakeholders that can impact transformative value and revenue value?
- Are our relationships with our stakeholders defined clearly enough to allow us to understand the impacts of changes caused by those stakeholders?
- Can we decrease the number of stakeholders within our transformative value chain?
- Can we decrease the risks and complexities within our transformative value chain?

The Executive View: Innovation Is Very Risky

Executive teams often have a difficult time quantifying the benefits and return on investment in pursuing a particular invention/innovation cycle. This is especially true when the invention/innovation cycle is an attempt to enhance an existing product that is in the latter stages of the innovation life cycle. At these latter stages of negative and destructive invention, it often appears as if the price of product consumption is in a complete free fall, cheaper-priced competitive products are arising, and consumer satisfaction (transformative value) is plummeting.

As we have seen, each of these symptoms can be caused by one or more of the perceived randomness factors, product commoditization, or shifts within the transformative value chain. These causes are often so interwoven and difficult to identify that there appear to be only two options:

- Decrease costs in order to decrease price, increase transformative value, and increase revenue value.

- Deliver new positive disruptive or incremental innovations that increase transformative value and revenue value.

The problem that executives have with the second option (new innovation) is that previous attempts at new product innovation have delivered negative incremental inventions or even destructive inventions. Choosing to pursue even more "innovation" on the existing product space in these circumstances is often summarized as "throwing good money after bad."

In general, innovation consultants will instruct the executive team that they must increase risk taking in order to counteract this downward plunge. Unfortunately, unless the current causes of the downward plunge are identified, increased risk is most likely to produce additional failures.

At the end of Chapter 3 we briefly discussed the optimal innovation life cycle as depicted in Figure 3.10. An increase in risk taking by the executive team as a means of reversing the innovation life cycle will run head on into the natural flow of the life cycle, as depicted in Figure 5.7. An executive mandate that is not based on an increased understanding of the current causes and symptoms within the innovation life cycle is very likely to fail. It is this apparent continuation of a random approach to innovation that causes many executives to reject increased risk taking as a solution and pursue cost reductions instead.

In Chapter 6 we will discuss how to eliminate the need for increased executive risk taking in order to deliver new product innovations.

BOB SHOULD CONSIDER

- Can we isolate the causes of the apparent decline of the transformative value of our products?
- Is it potentially damaging to aggressively attempt to reduce costs as well as develop new innovations?
- If an executive mandate is required, what should it be based on?

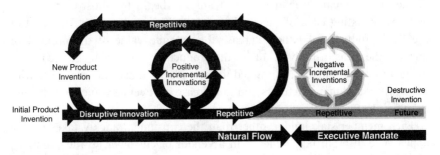

FIGURE 5.7 Increase in risk taking

Management Team Challenges with Incremental Innovation

As the product delivery chain is initially constructed, management teams will create the transformative value/revenue value relationships for each stakeholder within the product delivery chain. Some of these relationships might include the following:

- **Supplier:** Pricing schedules that decrease as purchase volumes increase. This initially maximizes the revenue value to the supplier and creates an acceptable transformative value to the company. Over time, the relationship will likely shift decreasing revenue value to the supplier while increasing transformative value to the company.

- **Manufacturer:** Trial production run at higher purchase price with lower per production run costs in the future.

- **Distributor:** Extremely favorable price terms to initial distributors, giving them the best competitive position if the product sales increase.

- **Value-added reseller:** First market entrant status will allow the VARs to become the dominant provider within their market niches.

- **Installer:** Little or no start-up costs through free training, equipment, and so on.

Each of these initial relationships is designed to maximize both the transformative value and revenue value of the relationships between the respective parties in order to get commitments from all the stakeholders. These commitments are necessary in order to maximize the transformative value to the consumer and to drive the consumer to purchase the product.

Once the product delivery chain is completed and as the product comes to market, the company's management team will begin to adjust costs downward by adjusting each of these relationships. This will decrease the cost of the final product and either increase the revenue value of the product or increase the transformative value of the product, or both. Each change implemented by the company is designed to increase its transformative value with its suppliers and manufacturers and to increase its revenue value with the distributors, VARs, installers, and consumers.

Each member stakeholder, other than the consumer, quickly takes on the appearance of a partner, rather than a vendor or customer, to the company. This effectively hides all external views of the relationships from the company. It is no longer deemed critical to maintain the revenue value to the suppliers or to maintain the transformative value to the deliverers (distributors and so on). The only relationship that remains critical in the eyes of the product management team is the transformative value/revenue value relationship with the consumer.

At this final stage, all views of transformative value have been shifted to the consumer, effectively eliminating the overlaps of the product delivery chain and the transformative value chain. Figure 5.8 depicts this relationship between the company and the product delivery chain stakeholders.

Once this compression of the transformative value chain has occurred in the minds of the product management team, it is extremely difficult for the team to find new innovations. Most assumptions will be based on the existing product delivery chain and that it has been optimized to the fullest. Any new innovations will be deemed to require an increase in the transformative value of the consumer. By ignoring the innovation potentials throughout the product delivery chain, the management team is dramatically reducing the options and the intellectual property that can be brought to bear to create new innovations.

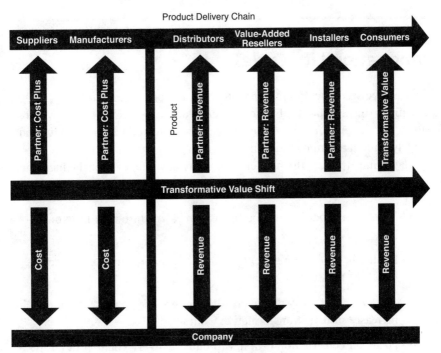

FIGURE 5.8 Compression of the transformative value chain

We will see in Chapter 6 how the management team can realign the product delivery chain and the transformative value chain to restart the innovation life cycle.

BOB SHOULD CONSIDER

- Have we reduced our suppliers' costs (and decreased the suppliers' revenues) to an extent that our "partners" now view our supplies as commodities with no value in new innovations?

- Have we increased our revenues from our deliverers (distributors and so on), and inversely reduced their revenues, to an extent that our "partners" now view our product as a low margin commodity with little potential for innovation?

- Have we compressed the transformative value chain and centered all innovation potential on the target consumer market that has probably already entered commoditization?

Competitor's Advantages Within the Innovation Life Cycle

As we have seen, the natural tendency of most companies is to maximize the benefit to the company of any partner relationships. This tendency drives down the revenues of the partners, tends to commoditize the product, and largely eliminates innovation on the part of the partners.

New competitors to the market have many advantages over the incumbent company:

- New, more modern product delivery infrastructure with little or no legacy costs

- Minimum costs from suppliers and manufacturers thanks to incumbent cost pressures

- Ability to lure away deliverers (distributors and so on) with minimal increases in their transformative values

- Focus on construction of a new product delivery chain with all the attendant innovation potentials

- Delivery of a "good enough" product, without all the weight of previous negative incremental and destructive inventions

- Ability to increase transformative value to existing consumer base through both price cuts and new innovations

- Little or no R&D costs to amortize

- Overall better margins than incumbent competitors

In many ways, new competitors enter the market like a new farmer walks onto existing cropland bought out of bankruptcy. The land has been plowed, weeded, and planted and is under harvest. All the competitor has to decide is what new crops to plant going forward. And so, the innovation life cycle is restarted.

We will discuss in Chapter 6 how to minimize the opportunities for new competitors while maximizing the innovation potential of the incumbent company.

BOB SHOULD CONSIDER

- Are we creating the perfect environment for new competitors?
- How can we take advantage of the same opportunities as our new competitors?
- Does the fact that the new competitor is "new" have an impact on its success?
- Do we need to become "new" through management changes, changing innovation policies, and so on?

All of these pressures accumulate and drive the product team to focus inside the box. Thinking outside the box becomes very dangerous. It is almost a knee-jerk reaction, not unlike flipping that light switch in a power failure or blowing on cold noodles. The team doesn't consciously avoid looking outside the box. They are conditioned to look only inside.

Bob Should Consider

- How can we stop building the blasted box?
- If our team is stuck looking inside the box, how can we change this?
- How can we avoid building the box altogether?

Assumptions Everywhere

If I had to use one word to describe virtually all of the limitations that companies have when it comes to being able to innovate, that word would be *assume* and all its forms. Sometimes the assumption is hard to recognize and find. But, if you look deep enough, you will find it. So, why is *assume* such a deadly word for innovation?

Here are three examples of some of the many statements I have heard in the last year that reek of assumptions. Each of these statements was actually killing innovation within the respective companies:

- "Our equipment provider is very slow to integrate our functional requirements. This really limits our ability to deliver new product features quickly to market."

- "Our existing product has almost commoditized, so we are reducing our staff and looking around to acquire a new product line."

- "Our customers' needs have shifted away from our product."

These seem like perfectly logical and reasonable statements. And in some cases they may be quite accurate. But, relative to the particular companies I was speaking to, the following were the actual underlying assumptions for each statement:

- The company was assuming that the only way to deploy certain aspects of its product was through integration performed by the equipment provider. As the company drove down costs, it also reduced the revenue value of the product relative to the equipment provider. The equipment provider no longer had the revenue value to justify working aggressively with the company.

- The company was assuming that there was no longer any possibility to harvest new revenues from the existing product line and that the only way to replace declining revenues was through acquiring a completely new product line and revenue stream.

- The assumption is that the transformative value of the product to existing customers has fallen to zero. This could be true in the event that a new disruptive innovation has shifted the customers to an alternative market. But, most likely the revenue value has fallen too far, and all attempts at innovation are yielding negative or destructive results.

If the statements actually did reflect an underlying assumption, how should the companies have looked at each situation? Here are the actual results of questioning the statements:

- The company had three choices: 1) proceed with the unsatisfactory relationship with the equipment vendor, ignoring the negative impacts on product delivery schedules, 2) increase the revenue value of the product to the equipment provider by increasing the price the company paid the equipment provider, or 3) treat the equipment provider as a component provider and have someone else develop an add-on that could satisfy the needs of the product road map in a timelier manner. The company chose option 3, which simplified its relationship with the equipment vendor, reduced costs overall, and returned control of the product delivery chain to the company. The company was able to innovate.

- This is the typical inside-the-box management viewpoint. In reality, the company had tremendous value opportunities within its product delivery chain that could be used for new products as well as the old. By killing this and several other assumptions, the company was able to harvest the intellectual property/intrinsic value created throughout the product history and create a new disruptive product that made use of the existing product delivery chain. With additional tweaking to the existing product delivery chain, costs were reduced for the original product line allowing a price reduction that resulted in increased sales. The new product line utilized the increases in economies of scale and was an instant disruptive innovation in an alternative market.

- This is the typical innovation life cycle late-stage comment. Since no disruptive innovation had completely shifted the customer base to a new market, the decreased sales and revenues were caused by increased complexity and price brought on by negative and destructive attempts to create new innovations. By recognizing that this shift had occurred, the company was able to simplify its product to a "good enough" version, reduce the development staff, cut costs, and slash prices. The product's transformative value quickly rose, and the product's penetration expanded into previously untapped market segments.

Killing assumptions is one of the best ways to eliminate the "box" limitations on innovation capabilities of an existing product team. This can seldom be done with internal team members. An objective external viewer has no loyalties to previous decisions or deployments. The previous three examples demonstrate three assumptions that many product teams make:

- **Assumption 1:** Innovations do not include changing the product delivery chain. In reality, the product delivery chain can be adjusted at will to deliver new innovations. In this example, the "box" excludes the product delivery chain as a source of new innovative product improvements.

- **Assumption 2:** The intellectual property/intrinsic value to the company of a legacy product resides in the product itself. In reality, the product delivery chain has inherent values that can be translated into new products as well as enhancements of the existing product. In this example, the "box" does not recognize processes as intellectual property with value available for new innovations.

- **Assumption 3:** Any drop in transformative value is a result of poorly understood changes in the consumer's lifestyle. In reality, absent a disruptive innovation, the drops in transformative value are probably caused directly by the company and its competitors. In this example, the "box" views the consumer/product relationship very simplistically and does not take into consideration the transformative value chain.

There are probably as many ways to hide an assumption as there are leaves in a forest. And it can be quite frustrating for a team to attempt to internally isolate these assumptions. Imagine saying "Why is that true?" after each and every statement that a team member makes in a planning session.

External facilitators who can recognize the broad, hidden, and dangerous assumptions are often the best option for quickly turning around a product innovation team. Each of the previous cases was resolved quickly once the assumption was eliminated.

To isolate assumptions and remove them as roadblocks to innovation, follow these steps:

1. Define each issue or pain point that restricts product success.

2. State that the existing solution, the one creating the issue or pain point, is no longer available.

3. Define alternative solutions to replace the eliminated solution. These alternative solutions can include parts of the eliminated solution but cannot duplicate it completely.

4. Apply the lessons learned back on the existing solution.

If we take our three examples and apply these steps, we find the following:

- 1) The pain point is the equipment provider not delivering quickly what we need for our product. 2) We then eliminate the equipment vendor as a solution. 3) The alternative is to use a standard piece of equipment in conjunction with a new component. 4) We then apply this to our original provider, utilize its standard product, and attach a new component.

- 1) The pain point is that our product has almost commoditized. 2) We eliminate staff reductions and acquire a new product as the solution. 3) The alternative is to harvest all intellectual and process value from the existing product and then target that value with enhancements at a new market, thus benefiting both products. 4) We then apply this to the original product, which allows us to cut costs, decrease prices, increase transformative value, and restore sales for the original product.

- 1) The pain point is that our sales have dropped and customer satisfaction is low. 2) We eliminate the assumption that our customers need for our product is shrinking. 3) Instead, we conclude that we can eliminate the negatives in the product and deliver a "good enough" version that is cheaper to maintain and deploy. This allows us to cut

> **BOB SHOULD CONSIDER**
>
> - Do we understand what drives the consumer's transformative value for our product?
> - Can we utilize both the physical and intrinsic transformative value factors to create new innovative products?
> - How can we create a driver of transformative value that is independent of the actual product?

Product Delivery Chain Stakeholders

As we discussed in Chapter 5, the product delivery chain will consist of one or more stakeholders other than the consumer. These stakeholders may be both internal and external to the company.

One of the greatest mistakes that companies seem to make when attempting to create or deploy a new product innovation is to only consider the consumer's transformative value. This is a major mistake since the other stakeholders can have a dramatic negative impact on the success of the product.

Often, when I ask companies about innovating new products and the relationship of the various stakeholders, they almost immediately start "talking in circles." This is understandable since the stakeholders are separate pieces of the product delivery chain and each stakeholder is intertwined with the others. It is difficult to separate the stakeholders as stand-alone when they are part of an integrated whole.

I have found that the simplest approach to correcting the transformative value chain is to view each stakeholder in the chain as the *only* member of the chain. In other words, look at the supplier completely alone. Then look at the manufacturer completely alone. Then follow in stages with the distributor, the value-added reseller, the installer, and finally the consumer.

For instance, assume that the "distributor" is the final purchaser of the product as far as the company is concerned. It doesn't matter what the distributor does with the product. We don't care if the distributor just places it in a warehouse. Using this assumption, we can then ask, "What is the transformative value of the product to the distributor, and how can I increase it to the maximum value?" This will allow us to understand how to properly balance the company's relationship with the distributor.

If we return to our pharmaceutical example, the distributor would be an insurance company or other form of payee like a government agency. We would need to determine how to maximize the transformative value to the insurance company so that the insurance company would want to purchase the drug product for its customers. This might involve additional justifications, long-term pricing arrangements, or other incentives outside of just demonstrating the efficacy of the drug.

Once we have completed determining the best way to balance the transformative value with the distributor, we could then move on and do the same process for the value-added reseller. In the pharmaceutical example, this might be the doctor. We need to enhance the doctor's ability to practice medicine, increase the doctor's revenue through billable events of the therapy, decrease the amount of time per patient, and so on.

Continuing with this process would allow us to maximize the transformative value chain for all stakeholders while also stabilizing and guaranteeing our product's flow into the market.

Even in the case of a simple consumer good, such as a box of dried mashed potatoes, there is still quite a complex product delivery chain and a corresponding transformative value chain. Any negative shifts in the transformative value chain for any of the stakeholders can cause the product to stop being distributed, sold, and consumed.

7

The Innovation Checklist

We have discussed a great many concepts from the differences between an invention and an innovation to how all members of the product delivery chain actually share a transformative value and revenue value relationship. Now let's summarize and discuss how to resolve problems with the innovation life cycle.

In this chapter, we will discuss a checklist that can be used in virtually all companies with any product. In Part III of the book, we will apply this checklist to your company's particular situation.

Overview of the Innovation Checklist

In Chapters 1 through 6, I laid out many of the problems that can align to stifle innovation within otherwise successful companies. In these companies, the innovation life cycle proceeds merrily along toward ultimate product commoditization because management teams make what seem to be all the right decisions along the way driven by competitors, revenue requirements, customer needs, and more.

Each company is unique. Each product is unique. Each market is unique. And each innovation life cycle is unique. Therefore, it is probably impossible to describe an all-encompassing magic formula that will restart the innovation life cycle in all circumstances of products, markets, and companies. However, we can take certain steps to isolate and understand our particular circumstances. These steps are summarized in a checklist form here and will be applied for differing competitive viewpoints in the following chapters. The sequence of the checklist items is not as important as simply accomplishing them.

The innovation checklist consists of the following items:

- Isolate the drivers of the consumer's transformative value.
- Fully understand your product delivery chain.
- Align the different viewpoints within your company.
- Isolate pain points in the product delivery chain.
- Reenergize the transformative value chain.
- Define a "good enough" product.
- Seize control of push-me/pull-you.
- Kill assumptions.
- Recognize your innovation life cycle stagnation.
- Figuratively commoditize your product.
- Isolate intellectual property.
- Map intellectual property to new markets.
- Create disruptive innovations.
- Fund disruptive innovation.

Isolate the Drivers of the Consumer's Transformative Value

I love some of the commercials on TV these days. There is one that talks about a candy bar being the perfect afternoon energy booster. I am sure that there is a segment of the viewing public that latches onto this premise and uses it to justify, at least in their own minds, why they munch down on a candy bar every afternoon. I just eat the candy bar because I love it.

If we drill down deeper into that candy bar's consumer market, we would probably find that the drivers of the transformative value of the candy bar don't include "healthy" or "energy" anywhere in the top ten drivers. And, unfortunately for the advertiser, the premise of being an "afternoon energy booster" can be universally applied to all candy bars, so there is no uniqueness in the candy bar being advertised this way. Why would one candy bar (and I am excluding "energy bars" from the candy bar category) deliver more energy than the next candy bar? Sugar is sugar.

So, why is the manufacturer advertising the "afternoon energy" linkage? It is probably trying to eliminate or reduce the guilt we are made to suffer these days about simple pleasures. It probably won't be long before we see advertisements for candy bars that push "organic," "green," or even "economically revitalizing." But, regardless of the advertiser's intentions, the basic transformative value of the product probably remains unchanged.

In the case of the candy bar in question, the drivers of the transformative value probably include items such as these:

1. **Chocolate**: Satisfies chocolate lovers

2. **Caramel**: Satisfies caramel lovers

3. **Peanuts**: Satisfies peanut lovers

4. **Cost**: Relatively inexpensive

5. **Convenience**: Easy to carry and easy to eat even in busy situations

6. **Acceptable**: Generally acceptable to eat even in meetings, parties, or other public functions

There are probably other, more subtle drivers of the candy bar's transformative value, but this list will suffice for now.

Now, let me ask you a couple of questions. When you are in the store standing in front of a bunch of candy bars, do you ever think "Which one will energize me the most?" When you are selecting a soft drink from a soda machine, do you ever think "I want the Real Thing?" Or do you just buy the one that you feel in the mood for at that time?

The point is that marketing is sometimes not targeted at the underlying transformative value of the product at all. I think the best candy bar commercials are the ones where they slowly pull the candy bar in half. Yum!

When trying to understand why a product is commoditizing or sales are dropping off, it is very critical that you return to the foundational reasons that consumers bought the product in the first place. Go back and document what the transformative value of the product was in the beginning, and then evolve the product and its transformative value forward into the present day. You need to understand why (or in many cases "if") the transformative value has fallen. Then you can remove those drivers from the transformative value.

In the case of the candy bar, perhaps chocolate has become extremely expensive because of a fungus damaging the cocoa bean crop several years ago. To avoid increasing the price, your company adjusted the formula. Consumer response seemed to be acceptable, so the formula was never changed back even though the price of cocoa fell back to normal levels the next season. Then perhaps your company shifted from sugar to corn syrup, again to reduce costs. Over time, while making adjustments to protect the revenue value, perhaps you destroyed part of the transformative value.

If you have ever eaten a candy bar manufactured outside the United States, you probably know where I am leading. I ate a candy bar in China and almost fainted. It tasted fabulous! Why? Because it was made with sugar and not corn syrup. It wasn't as sweet and wasn't cloying like many corn syrup–based products. The same was true when I drank an orange soda. Wow! I would almost fly back to China just to taste those flavors again . . . they are not available in the U.S.-based versions of the same products.

Perhaps your transformative value of your product has fallen because you have forgotten why consumers buy your product. In the case of the candy bar, the number-one reason is probably taste. It's not convenience or energy or any other reason. Taste.

Checklist item #1: To understand why your product is where it is today, go back to where it was when it was most successful, and isolate the foundational transformative value of the product.

Fully Understand Your Product Delivery Chain

Your product was successful at some point and has commoditized over time. As we discussed in Chapter 6, this commoditization is a result of a complete shifting of the transformative value chain into the consumer's transformative value/revenue value relationship.

At the point that this shift occurs, your company will likely view the entire product delivery chain as a streamlined operation with little room for innovation. But, there can be innovation opportunities embedded throughout the product delivery chain that are hidden by assumptions.

The next couple of checklist items are dependent on a thorough understanding of your product delivery chain. This does not require a financial analysis, extensive research, or market analysis of each supplier or distributor. Instead, it is important to understand each player in the product delivery chain, their criticality to the final product, their impact on your company's flexibility, and your ability to gain increased innovation value from the relationship.

Checklist item #2: Review all of the partners in your product delivery chain. Label them as component suppliers or innovation suppliers, inhibitors or accelerators, and unique or one of many.

Align the Different Viewpoints Within Your Company

As we discussed in Chapters 4 and 5, there are many viewpoints within a company concerning the success or failure of a product. Most of these viewpoints are coming from participants within the product delivery chain who are internal to the company. Unfortunately, we rarely look at these as relationships in the same way we look at our relationships with external suppliers or distributors. But, the impact from internal relationships on the success of the product can be significantly worse than the impact from your external partner relationships.

When you were thinking in the previous part about understanding your product delivery chain, I'll bet you left out the internal relationships. This is all too common and is often the downfall of product innovation attempts. When these internal relationships are poorly understood and improperly managed, the "talking in a circle" phenomenon will likely never end.

It is critical to view all decision makers who can have an impact on delivery of the existing or new product as if they were separate partners who must be managed and who have a unique transformative value/revenue value relationship.

Checklist item #3: Include all the internal company players within your product delivery chain. Just as you did with your external partners, label them as component suppliers or innovation suppliers, inhibitors or accelerators, and unique or one of many.

Isolate Pain Points in the Product Delivery Chain

In the "slow supplier" example we discussed in Chapter 6, the slowness was a major pain point in the company's ability to deliver new product features to the market. These new features could result either in incremental innovations or even in disruptive innovations. But, the "slow supplier" assumption was probably dramatically impacting all aspects of any new product road maps and features.

The quickest way to isolate pain points is to assume that they will never get better. People take a pain reliever for a headache when they finally reach the conclusion that the headache isn't going to go away any other way. We moan and groan that our head hurts, and then the normal reply from our friends is, "Did you take something for it?"

Isolating product delivery pain points is just about as simple. In the case of my client and the "slow supplier," my client was constantly looking for ways to speed up the supplier. The client never looked for alternative solutions because the client assumed the supplier could be "fixed." Over time, however, as my client continued to shift the transformative value/revenue value relationship away from the supplier's favor, the situation only got worse.

Checklist item #4: Isolate your product delivery chain pain points. Assume that these pain points will soon become infinitely worse. Commoditize the relationship, and find alternatives.

Reenergize the Transformative Value Chain

As we discussed in Chapter 6, the success of your product came from the give-and-take of all of your suppliers, distributors, and other participants of your product delivery chain. Through the evolution of your product, you have most likely maximized your revenue value of all relationships in the corresponding transformative value chain. In the process, you have reduced the transformative value to your "partners" and have likely commoditized the relationship in their eyes.

To understand how your product reached its current state and to understand how to innovate new products from it, you must understand which relationships have been commoditized in "appearance only." If the relationship is truly commoditized—for instance, when the component you are purchasing is commoditized—then there is little risk from competitors utilizing that relationship against you. If, however, the relationship is only commoditized because you have destroyed the transformative value/revenue value relationship, then your competitors can utilize the same relationship in a potentially far more productive manner than you are doing today.

By looking back at the transformative value chain and determining, albeit hypothetically, how you could adjust the transformative value/revenue value relationship more in favor of your partners, you will likely be able to identify new ways that those partners can provide increased value to your product's consumers.

Checklist item #5: Document your product's transformative value chain, and determine which relationships have been restricted by shifts within the transformative value/revenue value relationship.

Define a "Good Enough" Product

One of the underlying principles throughout this book is the concept of positive incremental innovations versus negative incremental inventions. The primary delineator of when positive starts to shift toward negative is when the concept of a "good enough" product is surpassed.

Companies have the tendency to always pursue the bigger customers, the bigger contracts, and the bigger revenue opportunities. In the process, their products will start to become focused on the needs of specific large customers and will leave the smaller consumers in the market behind. At first blush, this makes perfect business sense. Why sell 500 copies of a software package to small to medium-size companies when you can sell one copy to a very large enterprise?

The problem with this approach is that you are accomplishing the following by focusing ever upward within the market:

- You are targeting your product, and your company, at an ever-shrinking niche market.

- Your ability to increase revenues is based on your ability to continuously drive up the transformative value of your product to the same large customers.

- Your product is becoming increasingly complex and more difficult to evolve and support.

- Your product is becoming specialized for the unique needs of a few dominant customers.

- Your infrastructure and product delivery chain are focused toward meeting the needs of a niche market.

- You are opening up the bottom of the market to new competitors that can steal your product's transformative value cheaper than you can retain it.

There are probably many other negatives to pursuing the normal shift up the market ladder without considering retention and dominance of the lower layers of the market.

To innovate new products from your existing product, you must understand what constitutes a "good enough" product throughout the existing market. Obviously, the larger companies will still want their special features. But, if these special features were not available, they would settle for good enough.

Think back to the candy bar example. There are undoubtedly some consumers who view a particular candy bar as an "energy bar." Even without the additional branding as an energy bar, the candy bar itself probably constitutes a "good enough" product that the consumer is likely to purchase anyway.

It is critical that you dissect your product, at least figuratively, in order to understand how your product compares to this "good enough" product definition. Your ability to control and dominate a market and to remain in control will rely largely on your delivery of a universally "good enough" product that can be enhanced for the niche markets without damaging the "good enough" foundation.

After all this talk of candy bars, you are probably ready to go grab a candy bar. But, here is one more candy bar example: Mounds and Almond Joy. They are basically both chocolate-covered coconut bars, with Almond Joy being a niche version with almonds. The slogan is the perfect "good enough" example: "Sometimes you feel like a nut, sometimes you don't." The point is that the "good enough" product still exists for all lovers of chocolate-covered coconut. If you happen to also love almonds, Hershey's has the niche product for you. It has maintained the foundational transformative value of the product to maintain control of the entire market and enhanced that transformative value for some consumers.

Checklist item #6: Determine what a "good enough" version of your product is—not for your existing customer base but for all customers within the market. Assume that there would be no competitors so everyone would have to buy the "good enough" version. You can then add on to the "good enough" versions in a nondestructive way to control the niche market segments against competition.

Seize Control of Push-Me/Pull-You

As we discussed in Chapter 4, the push-me/pull-you competitive pressures can distort your product's features, target market, and resulting transformative value. It is critical that your company seize control of this push-me/pull-you cycle and respond only in ways that are beneficial to your company, your product, and your consumer. Otherwise, you will quickly drive your product beyond "good enough" and open it up to aggressive competition.

One of the best ways to control the push-me/pull-you competition is to analyze all competitive products and to define the transformative value differences between your competitors' products and your own product. Utilizing this comparison, you can do the following:

- Control the incremental innovation of the marketplace

- Deliver incremental innovations that both maximize your transformative value while negatively impacting the transformative value of your competitor's products

- Patent incremental innovations prior to delivery to market in an attempt to increase the longevity of your market position

- Ignore competitive product features that do not contribute to your good enough product or increase the consumer's transformative value

- Decrease negative feature responses by monitoring the transformative value impact of your competitors' new features

The goal is to shift the push-me/pull-you model into more of a push-you/pull-you model. Such a push-you/pull-you model allows you to react in the most positive manner available to the actions of each competitor. The larger the number of competitors, the more likely you are to control the market through a transformative value comparison and management model.

Checklist item #7: Step away from the normal push-me/pull-you model and toward a transformative value comparison and management model.

Kill Assumptions

I won't fully repeat the "You know what assume means" story that appears in half the sports-related movies on the planet. But, it is just as true here when discussing innovation. And as we discussed in Chapter 6, assumptions can be extremely hard to identify and to eradicate. Many of the other checklist items are specifically designed to eliminate the bad assumptions and to add assumptions that force you to consider different solutions to those you already make use of.

One of the biggest problems with assumptions is that they can be layered one on top of the other until the original assumptions are buried from view. We discussed briefly the impact of assumptions in Chapter 2 on market size and transformative value. These assumptions can then drive product features, costs, sales methods, marketing, and many other aspects of product delivery in the completely wrong directions. Finding these layers of assumption can be challenging since the person questioning the top-layer assumptions is often classified as "that idiot who doesn't understand our business." I have had more than my share of clients resist this requirement right up until we find the foundational assumption that was totally wrong. Then they are shocked at how simple solving their innovation issues becomes.

As I mentioned earlier, killing assumptions is one of the key areas that I have found most challenging for my clients. It takes almost a complete discounting of everything they have come to treat as "firm reality" for them to isolate the assumptions. A facilitator in this area is often money extremely well spent.

Checklist item #8: If you find yourself going in circles or running into an insurmountable problem, then you probably have an underlying assumption that is killing you. Turn it around, and kill all assumptions.

Recognize Your Innovation Life Cycle Stagnation

Once you have determined what constitutes a "good enough" product, you will need to keep this definition current throughout the evolution of the market. Your competitors, or even your own product innovations, could cause the market to shift and in the process change the definition of a "good enough" product.

As you define new product features to deliver to market, you must continuously map these back to the "good enough" product definition. You never want to over-innovate the baseline product. Otherwise, you are forcing the innovation life cycle into negative territory.

If you are developing/selling different versions of your product to target specific niche markets, then you should maintain multiple "good enough" definitions as well as multiple transformative values, one for each niche market. It is all too common for these features, targeted at a specific customer or market, to become rolled into the baseline product as a requirement for the entire market. This is the point that the product starts to become too complex and surpasses the baseline "good enough" definition.

If the new feature is targeted at a particular niche within the market, then you should compare its worth to the niche market, not the whole market. You must not increase your perceived revenue value for the entire market based on features that have little or no transformative value to the entire market.

By tracking product changes to these baseline "good enough" product and transformative value definitions, you should be able to quickly recognize when you are pushing your innovation life cycle into negative or destructive territory.

Checklist item #9: The definition of a "good enough" product and transformative value for the entire market is critical to maintaining the positive side of the innovation life cycle. Never combine niche features with the "good enough" product definition.

Figuratively Commoditize Your Product

When attempting to find a new innovation, either disruptive or incremental, it is often difficult to step outside the box of the current product. Discussions will inevitably return to existing product road maps, customer commitments, competitive positioning, and the whole gambit of topic areas swirling around an existing product. These swirling topic areas can act as a whirlpool that sucks down and destroys all new ideas for product innovations.

To eliminate these distractions (and any more storm metaphors), I have found that it is best to figuratively commoditize the existing product. In other words, drive your perceived value of your existing product and its features to a fully commoditized level.

Figurative commoditization eliminates the circular product debates that often derail or severely confuse new product innovation attempts. When all existing parts/features/components become equally usable and flexible, it is much easier to locate new product inventions and to determine whether they are worth pursuing.

The clearest view of figurative commoditization is to view all existing features as if they were "black boxes" that can be utilized in any way desired. In essence, these black boxes become another component from an internal supplier within the new products delivery chain.

Companies often try to eliminate the need for figurative commoditization by establishing a completely new group responsible for product innovation. Although this does eliminate the collision between old and new, it will also often create an innovation team that is less broad and experienced than the original product team. If the existing team can follow through on figurative commoditization, it will be much simpler and cost effective to extend the resources to the existing team (from other areas within the company) to include product innovation.

Checklist item #10: Eliminate problems related to existing product decomposition and feature isolation from the new product innovation process by figuratively commoditizing and componentizing the existing product.

Isolate Intellectual Property

Many companies find it extremely difficult to isolate the intellectual property contained within their products. The most common cause for this that I have seen has to do with the way in which different features/components within the product are integrated together.

If the features/components have been integrated in a very structured, well-delineated fashion, it is much easier to recognize the intellectual property value of a particular feature/component. This often describes a relatively new product that has not gone through a great deal of incremental change.

If the features/components have been developed one on top of the other with little regard for delineation, it can be extremely hard to isolate and separate them. This is very common in many product categories including software, hardware, drugs, and even food items. These products are often older products that have evolved over time, often in the wrong directions, and have suffered extreme push-me/pull-you pressures.

In the latter, poorly delineated case, I have found that the easiest way to find intellectual property is to ignore the actual architecture or organization of the product and to focus on the features within the product. By making the assumption that the product can be easily decomposed into constituent parts, even if it cannot be, the features naturally become discussion areas that can be branded as intellectual property or not and that can be recombined into new products. The cost of and decision to actually decompose the legacy product can then be evaluated separately from the innovation process.

Checklist item #11: Isolate the functional concepts within your product in order to identify intellectual property. Ignore the difficulties and risks during the new product innovation process. Then balance the actual costs against the benefits of identified product innovations.

Map Intellectual Property to New Markets

Assuming that you are not trying to create a new disruptive product from scratch, then you will likely have some intellectual property that you can use competitively in other markets. Our Jelly Belly example we discussed in Chapter 6 is a great example of simple intellectual property that can be applied to alternative markets.

Continuing the Jelly Belly example, we might have determined that Jelly Belly's intellectual property includes the following:

- Formulas for diverse flavors

- Packaging and delivery technologies for manufacturing and delivering flavors

- A marketing concept revolving around personal flavor creation

Jelly Belly could then look at potential markets where personal flavor creation is not already present and where the consumer would probably find a high transformative value in blending their own flavor product. It is not important at this stage to actually be able to deliver a product but rather to identify the market and transformative value for a product should it be created and delivered in the future.

The personalized flavor concept could readily apply to the following markets with high potential transformative values:

- **Yogurt:** Utilizing unflavored yogurt as a base

- **Soft drinks:** Utilizing club soda as a base

- **Ice cream:** Utilizing vanilla ice cream as a base

In each of these markets Jelly Belly would not need to become a competitor with existing product manufacturers. There are already "unflavored" (or mild vanilla) product varieties in each market. Jelly Belly could utilize its existing intellectual property to become a major flavor competitor within the marketplace through selling multiflavor crystals.

Checklist item #12: Do not attempt to innovate a new product first. Instead identify potential markets that will maximize the utilization of the company's existing intellectual property.

Create Disruptive Innovations

I am sure you have heard sayings like "There is nothing new under the sun" or "Everything has already been invented."

In many ways, these sayings are correct. As we discussed in Chapter 1, there are foundational inventions that are then utilized throughout a stream of new inventions and innovations. Most new disruptive product innovations are combinations of one or more existing inventions acting as black-box components that are blended together into a new product offering with perhaps a smattering of new innovation. The result is a new product that delivers lifestyle impacts in new ways and garnishes a new transformative value from the consumers.

With this black-box approach to disruptive innovation, it is much easier to identify potential markets and products that might allow the creation of a disruptive innovation. The black boxes that you should consider first are your own intellectual property as well as your figuratively commoditized components. These can then be combined with new technologies or other black-box inventions that perhaps the company will acquire through purchase, through licensing, or from a supplier should the final product go to market.

Many people like to innovate the product and then identify the market. I find this approach to often be a waste of energy and time since a great deal of thought is expended on a potential product that may not have a market with a positive transformative value. I prefer to use a baseline set of black boxes and then brainstorm about potential consumer/business lifestyle issues that could be positively impacted by this black-box suite. This allows the review of many potential markets and ideas in a very short time.

Similar to killing assumptions, I think it is also easier to do this type of disruptive innovation brainstorming utilizing external company resources to facilitate the discussions. Finding disruptive innovations can be even more complex when the potential markets and consumers are outside the realm of experience of the company's current markets.

Checklist item #13: You have two choices: Visualize new products and then try to identify markets, or visualize new markets and then identify new products. The baseline to use in either approach is the "black boxes" of the company's intellectual property and product features as well as external inventions and innovations.

Fund Disruptive Innovation

Disruptive innovations by definition create a new transformative value for the consumer. Within an existing market, disruptive innovations will often deliver simplification, enhancement, cost reduction, or some combination of these three. Within a new market, disruptive innovation most often delivers simplification and enhancement with cost reduction being an issue controllable by the company delivering the initial disruptive innovation.

Funding the development and deployment of disruptive innovations can be a scary, nerve-racking process. This is primarily because of all the negative issues like randomness that we have already covered. In a perfect world, the justification for funding a new disruptive product would be a straightforward business decision. It should never be a technology decision.

Understanding, documenting, and utilizing the transformative value of the target market, as well as the transformative value for any competitors within the market, should reduce the decision to the business decision level without excessive risk taking. If the final decision appears to be one of faith, then more due diligence needs to be done to fully understand all aspects of the other items on this checklist.

Checklist item #14: Funding a new disruptive product innovation should be a business decision without a need to increase risk.

PART III
Targeted Innovation

8

How to Innovate from Scratch

If you ask almost anyone, and I really do mean almost anyone, whether they have a great product idea, you will almost universally receive a resounding "yes." As a species, we are extremely creative.

But actually delivering a market creating innovation from that idea can be extremely challenging. In this chapter, we will discuss innovating from scratch assuming that there is no preexisting invention or innovation. We will apply the concepts of the innovation checklist to innovating from scratch.

Innovation Is Not Invention

As we discussed in Chapter 1, invention and innovation must be viewed from different perspectives. Something does not need to have a transformative value in order to be an invention. The same is definitely not true for an innovation. For the innovation, utilizing something like transformative value is the only gauge of how innovative the product is. Zero transformative value equals inventions. Positive transformative value equals innovations.

This book has touched briefly on the types of inventions and how to invent. But, the focus is on how to create an innovation, not an invention.

At least once a day I get a call from a start-up company that is seeking guidance on how to get investors interested in its products. Invariably the company has invested a great deal of money in the invention and now needs funding to "deliver our innovative products to market." Although this situation can often be repaired, I consider not having a targeted market with a well-defined transformative value to be the number-one reason that start-up companies fail. The start-up has focused almost exclusively on the invention process when it should have been constantly targeting a clearly defined market and innovation process.

So, don't read this chapter if you are looking for "how to invent." That is the topic for a completely different book.

BOB SHOULD CONSIDER

- Are we confusing the invention process and the innovation process?
- Are we keeping a firm focus on our target consumer market even during the lengthy product invention process?

Cool Is Not Enough

I have consulted with a great many companies that have spent millions creating a phenomenal product only to discover that there is no market for the product. The underlying concept is still "cool," and many would say, "Wow, I want that!" So, why isn't there a market? There are a lot of reasons that the cool product may not have a viable market. Fast food is a great example.

- **Cost:** The number-one reason that an invention is not an innovation is probably the cost of the product to the consumer. The cost of the product outweighs any transformative value the product may have. The gourmet hamburger comes to mind. People are rarely willing to pay $12 for a drive-thru hamburger no matter how fabulous it is.

- **Availability:** If the distribution channels for the product are too unstable, then the product will likely not penetrate the consumer's lifestyle. I grew up eating at one particular fast-food chain. I would go out of my way to go to its stores. When I moved to a different state, that chain didn't exist in those markets. After years of not eating there, I shifted my preferences. I still love its food, but I don't seek it out any longer because availability was too unpredictable.

- **Consistency:** The consistency of the quality and value of the product is critical for maintaining the transformative value. Fast food is based largely on consistency. If I go to the same vendor in three different cities, I want the food to be consistent. Otherwise, the transformative value of the product is unreliable, and I may not return.

- **Integration:** <u>The product needs to become an integral part of the consumer's lifestyle.</u> If the fast food is excellent but cannot be eaten (without a messy, near-fatal driving experience) on the go, then it is really not fast food. Really good tacos are a great example. You can buy them at drive-thru stores, but you often need to pull over to eat them. Their messiness does not allow them to easily compete with burgers and fries.

We will discuss a new fast-food item, micro-pizzas, later in this chapter when talking about how to innovate from scratch utilizing our innovation checklist described in Chapter 7. Some of the checklist items are not critical to innovating from scratch and not included in this chapter.

> **BOB SHOULD CONSIDER**
>
> - Have we fully considered the cost, availability, consistency, and integration issues in determining our product's innovativeness, its market potential, and the consumer's transformative value?

Isolating a Market for an Invention

Why is this section titled "Isolating a Market for an Invention"? Well, quite often companies fail to have a firm and complete definition of who its potential customers are. Rolls Royce knows that its potential customers are primarily the very wealthy. It doesn't target all car buyers. How many Rolls Royce car commercials or web ads have you seen? Yet, within that "very wealthy" market, different consumers will want to change the color of the exterior and interior, and there will be add-on features at increased costs.

Before you actually invent your product, you should have already isolated your target market and understood the factors that influence the transformative value of your product to the consumers in that target market.

However, assuming that you already have spent time and money on an invention and that you didn't predefine your target market, how can you isolate the market after the invention process? There are several approaches, but the one I have found the easiest to implement is the following:

1. As we discussed in Chapter 7, commoditize your product figuratively. I know you have not actually sold any of your product, but assume

that it is not the greatest thing since sliced bread. By commoditizing it, you will look at all features within the invention as equally valuable.

2. Isolate the major features that your invention can deliver, and then treat them as black-box components. This gives you the building blocks for a potential variety of markets.

3. Assume your invention doesn't exist. I know that is hard, but it is critical. By throwing away the invention, you are killing the assumptions of how your black-box features have been combined. Your final target market may not want that combination.

4. Utilize your black-box features to define the possible markets that could benefit from each feature.

5. Define a set of "good enough" products that would deliver maximum transformative value to each of the possible markets you identified. These products should include features, if necessary, that you do not provide in your invention today. In this way, you are divorcing the market's needs from your predefined product delivery chain.

6. Overlay your planned features onto the "good enough" products you have defined.

7. Based on the size of the target market, complexity of product delivery, and all the financial balancing acts, determine which products and markets are the most optimal fit for your existing invention.

8. Create a product road map that targets your existing product (with any potential enhancements or modifications) toward your selected market(s).

The previous process requires a completely open mind concerning your current invention, its status, and its potential markets. The steps in the previous process are designed to attempt to force you to break out of your "inventor" mold. This is extremely difficult for people internal to a start-up to accomplish. As such, this is another area where an external facilitator is probably required and optimal.

The greatest risk that start-ups face is that they have progressed too far down the invention cycle without creating a targeted market definition. The necessary time and funding needed to correct the invention to meet the needs of a target market could be beyond the remaining resources of the company.

This process is essentially forcing you to perform an isolation of the consumer's needs as described in the next section but limiting the scope of that isolation based on the investment you have already put into your invention.

In many of the cases where I have implemented an approach similar to the one described earlier, the final road map for taking the invention to a true market innovation does not require a product substantially different from the original conceived invention. However, the subtleties of the changes that the invention needs to undergo in order to become an innovation can be completely invisible without following a similar process.

BOB SHOULD CONSIDER

- Do we need an external facilitator in order to find our target markets?
- How can we functionally decompose our invention and create a black-box view?
- If we follow this market isolation process, what markets do we discover that we were not considering before?
- Have we already progressed beyond the point of no return so that we do not have the time or funding needed to adjust our invention to meet the needs of our identified target market? How do we respond?

Isolating a Consumer Need

Smartphones are quickly becoming an indispensible part of many consumers' everyday lifestyles. The easy access to information, maps, shopping, communications, and so on, can have a staggering impact on the priorities in a consumer's life. And yet, just a couple of years ago there were no smartphones.

Trying to isolate a single consumer need can be like playing a game of 20 questions (only with a whole lot more questions). Consumers rarely know where their needs lie beyond saving time and money and increasing convenience and enjoyment.

If you are trying to identify a consumer need without any foundational invention concepts, then the following has worked best for me. I often just close my eyes and start free thinking following this simple process.

- **Population group:** Break the population down into categories of people who have disposable funds to buy a product: retired, businesspeople, parents, soccer parent, teenagers, and so on. Pick one. It doesn't matter which one. You can always come back and pick a different one. The more you cycle through this process, the better you will become.

- **Pain point:** Break down the pet peeves of the group you picked one at a time. In other words, what do they complain about? Pick one pet peeve.

- **Impact point:** Isolate where they spend their time and money today relative to that pet peeve. Determine why it is a pet peeve. Is it inconvenient, unsafe, costly, and so on? Isolating the impact point is critical to targeting a potential market with a high transformative value.

- **What if:** Create "what if" scenarios that address the pet peeve and provide benefit within the consumer's impact point. You want the consumer to be willing to buy your product because they benefit from the product.

- **Visualize:** Try to visualize a product or process that could deliver the benefit that you have identified. Don't worry about if the technology exists to create what you are visualizing; just assume that the technology exists.

If you were a writer on a science-fiction show, you could create cool technologies of the future through a very similar process that might look like this:

- **Population group:** An Earth army is defending against an alien species attacking Earth.

- **Pain point:** An alien species is unharmed by traditional weaponry such as bullets and missiles. They simply reform from the remaining parts.

- **Impact point:** You have to get close enough to set them on fire and keep them on fire to kill them. This is a very dangerous perspective.

- **What if:** What if you could make a bullet or other projectile that accomplished the "keep them on fire" from a safe distance?

- **Visualize:** Think about creating a chemical-based bullet that when impacting the alien's skin creates a self-sustaining burning process. Or perhaps you could create an alien-flesh-eating virus that could be delivered by bullet?

Did you notice earlier that I said I would start "free thinking" using a process? I have never talked to an established inventor who did not follow some form of process. Free thinking and free association, at least from the point of view of finding market successful innovations, will simply not work in most cases without a process to target the "free thinking."

Some inventors create voluminous notebooks of ideas and then try to find a potential market. Some do basic research looking for foundation inventions that others then carry forward into market innovations. But, none of them appears to utilize a form of invention/innovation free association. Thomas Edison, whose record 1,093 patents remains unchallenged, followed extremely methodical methods to identify consumer needs and isolate the best product to meet that need.

Frankly, trying to find a new consumer need without some type of process is probably impossible. Lots of people will likely argue this point and say, "It just came to me!" More than likely they had already isolated the population, the pain point, and the impact point but had never considered that information gathering from the perspective of a process. Then their definition of a "what if" did appear to just come to them out of the blue.

The final stage in the process of isolating a consumer need, visualization, often requires the involvement of someone who is a specialist within the technologies of the "what if" areas. This is why many people who get "out-of-the-blue" inspirations often say, "I just need someone to help me create the product."

The risk for "out-of-the-blue" inventions is that they are seldom based on a concise review of the transformative value of the target market. The Spider Ladder keeps coming to mind! Before you spend a great deal of time in the visualization stage, you should isolate the drivers of the transformative value as discussed in the next section. Otherwise, you may be pursuing an invention with little or no real market value.

Bob Should Consider

- Do we have a process that we follow to isolate a consumer need? If so, what is it?
- Are our employees instructed in how to utilize a process to identify consumer needs?

Isolate the Drivers of the Consumer's Transformative Value

People love pizza. It is one of the most widely consumed foods in America and around the world. It is rarely considered to be a fast-food item like drive-thru hamburgers. In some downtown areas, pedestrians can buy a slice of pizza and eat it while walking between one meeting place or another. For the driving fast-food consumer, however, there is really very little opportunity to obtain a slice of pizza on the road. I'm not sure I have ever seen a drive-thru pizza restaurant. If pizza is one of American's favorite foods, why can't I find it as a fast-food item at the leading fast-food chains? (Please note that I am not sure what process of preparation would deliver the optimal product to the consumer. I am conjecturing about possibilities prior to starting the invention process.) Assuming that pizza can be delivered utilizing techniques similar to those for other fast foods, what would be the key factors making up the consumer's transformative value for a mini-pizza? A quick review of our own personal fast-food dining experiences would probably yield the following:

- Size: The product must be easy to handle.

- Messy: The product should not be overly messy.

- Flavor: It should have great Italian flavor in the meats, cheese, and sauce.

- Value: It shouldn't be all bread dough. It should be more meat and cheese than bread or sauce.

- Variety: It should be a range of toppings and sauces.

- Timeliness: The product must be ready quickly.

- Cost: The cost should be within the range of other fast-food meals.

If we assume these criteria to be the major factors within our potential consumer's transformative value, then we can deduce the following:

- Size: The size should probably be 1 to 3 inches, which is easy to handle and potentially bite size.

- Messy: Perhaps more of a calzone form of a mini-pizza will work best. There's minimal sauce. Or perhaps we want a thinner sauce that is quickly absorbed into the bread dough?

- **Flavor:** It should have stronger Italian flavorings and spices to enhance the smaller eating format and to minimize the sauce.

- **Value:** It should have high-quality meats and cheeses.

- **Variety:** It should have different sauces such as tomato sauce, olive oil, Alfredo, and so on, as well as different vegetables, meats, and cheeses.

- **Timeliness:** It should be available in two to three minutes maximum in order to keep the drive-thru line moving.

- **Cost:** With the smaller, bite-size format, it should be possible to deliver several mini-pizzas for the same price as a hamburger meal. All mini-pizzas in a single order would be the same—no mix and match.

Based on our high-level analysis of the factors that will impact the consumer's transformative value, our product should be a package of several mini-pizzas that are 1 to 3 inches in size, with perhaps a thin breading layer across the top to minimize the mess while not excessively increasing the bread content. It should have minimal sauce volume with several types available. Different varieties and high-quality toppings and spices that provide a strong Italian eating experience should be available. And, it must be able to be prepared in less than two minutes and be of high quality.

Define a "Good Enough" Product

Pizzas are one of those amazing foods that can be quickly customized to satisfy almost any appetite or flavor preference. Both meat lovers and vegetarians can all find their personal preferences given the right combination of sauce and toppings.

A "good enough" bite-size mini-pizza will be three of the old standbys of cheese, pepperoni, and mushroom. Baseline pricing should cover these three "good enough" versions. Any customization beyond this point could demand a price premium.

The basic standby "good enough" pizzas are likely to be the largest volume sold. It is critical that the quality and taste of these three baseline pizzas be broadly acceptable to the consuming public. To meet the flavor demands of niches, have packets of different pizza sauces available, Italian spices, and perhaps Parmesan cheese (at an extra cost). These independent add-ons would expand the "good enough" products into particular flavor niches while having little impact on the time of delivery and a positive impact on quality.

The bread product could be preprepared and frozen, including a bottom and a thinner top. Frozen, cooked ingredients could be placed into the frozen bread on demand and then steamed to thaw, soften, and prepare them for the customer.

Seize Control of Push-Me/Pull-You

Once a viable mini-pizza format is delivered to the market, it will undoubtedly be copied or morphed by every other fast-food provider in the industry. This will almost overnight create the push-me/pull-you environment we have discussed.

It is critical to maintain the "good enough" product line because it has a positive consumer response. By selling many varieties of toppings and sauces, you have addressed a great many niche markets from day one.

To seize control of push-me/pull-you, you could introduce new, broader target markets that are not necessarily traditionally served by pizza stores. These could include non-Italian flavorings such as barbeque sauces, teriyaki sauces, and even Mexican sauces. In this way, you can introduce new products that provide increased variety, require minimal changes to the product delivery chain, provide increased revenues due to the expansion beyond "good enough," and potentially create new competitive mechanisms against other fast-food market competitors.

You would definitely want to patent any machinery developed as part of the product preparation and delivery process as well as bread dough formulas, sauce formulas, and so on.

9

IT Solution Innovation

In Chapter 1 we briefly discussed the difference between an internal and an external invention. The delivery of virtually all external products will involve internal IT systems needed to manage and process the flow of information toward maximizing the external consumer's transformative value and the resulting revenues.

In this chapter, we will apply the concepts of the innovation checklist to internal IT solution innovation. As we shall see, improper management of IT innovation can directly impact product innovations and revenues.

Centralized and Decentralized IT

Virtually every large company I have worked with goes through a cycle that I call the Big Bang Cycle of IT. As a company grows and ages, the IT department follows a cycle similar to the following:

1. All IT functions for all corporate divisions are centralized.

2. Cost cutting begins since a centralized IT function should be cheaper than separate decentralized IT groups. Cuts reduce the centralized IT organization's ability to respond to requirements from individual divisions.

3. Divisions become unhappy with the turnaround time for new features and processes.

4. Divisions fight to decentralize IT and argue against funding a centralized IT since they cannot get the functionality they need. The divisions shortcomings are blamed on centralized IT.

5. IT functions are separated into the individual divisions. Bang!

6. IT solutions in each division begin to diverge from each other. Corporate operations begin to suffer, complexity begins to rise, and costs escalate.

7. Executive management becomes unhappy with the cost of decentralized IT.

8. The company's shortcomings (capital and operating expenditures) are blamed on decentralized IT.

9. Repeat starting at step 1. Collapse!

This cycle seems to repeat itself over a five- to ten-year period. A change in executive management can greatly accelerate the cycle since new executive management will attempt to shift the existing IT delivery model to decrease costs and/or increase product delivery flexibility.

It is important to understand that the decentralized IT model can also be equated with a partially outsourced IT model. Steps 5 and 6 in the previous cycle could consist of one or more outsourcing relationships rather than returning all control to the divisions. However, over time, these outsourced IT functions will begin to increase in cost and complexity and often act as part of the drivers for steps 7 through 9.

The Big Bang Cycle of IT helps to explain why the CIO position often has the highest turnover rate within large companies. But, there are also underlying aspects of the cycle that relate directly to the other areas we have discussed throughout this book, including the product delivery cycle and the transformative value chain. Just because IT may be considered an internal function does not make it any different from an external supplier when it comes to product delivery and transformative value.

For purposes of this discussion, we will assume that IT solutions do *not* include standard business practices such as payroll and human resource functions. Although these are critical to the functioning of any group, applying innovations to them will not necessarily impact the product delivery cycle or the transformative value chain for a particular product.

BOB SHOULD CONSIDER

- Where are we in the Big Bang Cycle of IT?
- How can we maximize the benefit to the company of a centralized IT organization and maintain that benefit?
- How can we deliver the functional benefits of decentralized IT while pursuing the cost benefits of a centralized IT?

Isolate the Drivers of the Consumer's Transformative Value

When it comes to IT functions, just who exactly *is* the consumer? In some cases it is the internal department responsible for delivering a particular product to market. In other cases, if IT provides infrastructure for the product's market, then it can also be the external consumer. So, IT consumers can be either internal, external, or both.

Regardless of whether the consumer is internal, external, or both, the services delivered by IT are likely a critical component in the product delivery chain. Without IT, the product might never make it to market or could arrive late with too few features to meet the consumer's needs.

IT should be viewed just like any other supplier. If the revenue benefit to the IT organization drops below a certain point, then the relationship will commoditize. The result will be decreased deliveries and extended delivery timelines. Although costs may have been reduced, the impact will also be negatively felt on product revenues as the product begins to lose its ability to compete and starts to enter the negative stages of the innovation life cycle.

Conversely, IT should view its consumers as both internal and external. If IT fails to deliver the platforms and resources needed by the product development group, then the transformative value of IT to the internal consumer will be negatively impacted. In addition, any negative impact on the internal consumer will also likely lead to an external consumer's transformative value being directly and negatively impacted.

Just like any member of the transformative value chain, IT's relationship must be maintained to ensure that IT has the proper revenue incentives to deliver the optimal value to the product delivery chain. If this relationship is not maintained, then the relationship will commoditize, and IT will quickly cease delivering optimal value to both the internal and external consumers.

The IT organization should ensure that it is properly reflected in all transformative value chains for each product and market. This is the only way to properly reflect the value of IT to the revenue generation side of the company. IT and the product groups need to maintain a positive revenue relationship that will allow IT to view the relationship positively and to deliver innovations in a timely manner.

When IT is not properly reflected in the transformative value chains, the Big Bang Cycle of IT will start to accelerate toward stage 5 (the Bang!) to decentralize IT into the divisions of the company.

BOB SHOULD CONSIDER

- Have we decreased the ability of our IT organization to meet the needs of the divisions?

- Does our IT organization map its services into the transformative value chains of the appropriate products?

- Do our current processes allow our IT functions to reflect direct profitability impact, or do we treat IT as a pure cost center?

Fully Understand Your Product Delivery Chain

When working with a company to reenergize its product innovation, I will create a product delivery chain diagram that lays out all of the key components required for product delivery. Invariably, the company will leave off internal IT functions on the first draft. This is another one of those very dangerous assumptions that can kill innovation.

In many ways, IT can be viewed as a component supplier to the internal consumer, and the internal consumer (the product development group) is acting as a channel partner that is delivering an enhanced product to the external consumer. This makes IT an integral part of the product delivery chain.

When a product division executive tells me, "I don't know what I get for my money from IT. I think I can buy it cheaper somewhere else," I immediately know that IT has done a poor job of maintaining its visibility within the product delivery chain.

I know what you IT folks are saying: Why am I assigning the blame to IT? Well, it is the supplier's responsibility to make sure the consumer understands what they are paying for and that the consumer is happy with the purchase.

When a consumer buys a Cadillac, the consumer knows exactly why they are buying a Cadillac. It's because Cadillac told them again and again what distinguishes its cars from other cars. IT has a similar responsibility.

Unfortunately, without a way of viewing consumer value such as the transformative value chain and a thorough product delivery chain, it is extremely difficult for IT to reflect its contribution to the revenue side of the product equation. This lack of a direct profitability linkage can also accelerate the Big Bang Cycle of IT into decentralization.

BOB SHOULD CONSIDER

- Do we consider IT when we are looking at our product delivery chain?
- Is our IT organization focused on merely responding to requests and not on maximizing IT's benefit throughout the product delivery chain?

Align the Different Viewpoints Within Your Company

The Big Bang Cycle of IT exists largely because of the lack of a clear linkage of IT with product revenues. It is very difficult to defend increased IT expenditures without such a linkage.

The IT organization should approach its existence just like any supplier. IT needs to ensure that all key decision makers understand how IT acts relative to each product delivery chain. This includes the following:

- **Is IT a component supplier or an innovation supplier?** IT needs to make sure that the perceived image is the one that IT wants to be perceived. Obviously, if IT is positioned as an innovation supplier, IT will become a critical part of the product delivery chain.

- **Is IT an inhibitor or an accelerator?** If IT is an inhibitor, then it needs to document why it is an inhibitor. This could be because of layoffs and cost cuts. If IT needs to be an accelerator, then, like any other supplier, IT must justify any changes to the transformative value chain and product delivery chain that will allow IT to become an accelerator.

- **Does IT deliver a unique service, or can it be replaced?** IT should continually position itself as a unique provider. This can be through economies of scale, handling product group overlaps, providing specialized knowledge resources, and so on.

IT must maintain control of these perceptions throughout the company. Otherwise, it will be difficult to counter the arguments for decentralization of IT functions. Bang!

BOB SHOULD CONSIDER

- Is our IT group a component supplier or an innovation supplier?
- Is our IT group perceived as an inhibitor or as an accelerator?
- Does our IT group deliver unique services, or is IT a one-of-many supplier?

Isolate Pain Points in the Product Delivery Chain

IT should constantly be performing a self-diagnosis on itself just like any other supplier should. If IT becomes the source of one or more pain points in the product delivery chain, then the product group will eventually attempt to componentize the relationship and layer on innovation suppliers from other sources, such as externally.

This componentization of the IT relationship is another driver that will shift the Big Bang Cycle of IT toward decentralization. If all that IT is supplying are component-level functionalities, then the product division can decide to do those component functions itself in a cheaper fashion without the need for the centralized overhead. Bang!

Reenergize the Transformative Value Chain

As we discussed in Chapter 7, over time the transformative value chain will shift the bulk of the transformative value to the end product consumer. The impact on IT, as a participant in this transformative value chain, is that the relationship between IT and the product group becomes commoditized.

Unfortunately, the product group rarely understands why a supplier, even internal IT, is not delivering IT innovations that are needed for a new product release fast enough. The assumption is that the supplier is happy with the current relationship and views it in the same critical fashion that the product group does. This is seldom the case.

Once the relationship has commoditized, the suppliers (in this case IT) view the innovation life cycle for that product's relationship to have reached its final negative conclusion. IT will be unlikely to dedicate increasingly scarce resources on this product since there is little or no justification through revenue increases.

IT can often reenergize the transformative value chain by isolating the services it is delivering to the particular product and documenting how those services are different from those delivered to the other product divisions. In other words, IT should treat the product group as a niche market and treat any feature enhancements as justifiable only within the product delivery chain of that product. This will help to maintain the viability of a centralized IT organization and drive the Big Bang Cycle of IT toward . . . Collapse!

BOB SHOULD CONSIDER

- Has our IT group been treating all divisions equally when it comes to feature value?
- What steps do we need to take to reenergize the transformative value chain for each of our product groups?
- Are we expecting innovation from our internal IT group without funding that innovation through a positive transformative value?

Define a "Good Enough" Product

Having worked with some extremely large companies with thousands of products, I have seen some horrendously bad IT implementations, especially in the areas of sales support, order processing, commissions, knowledge management, marketing, and customer support. Invariably these are centralized IT shops that have attempted to provide a single system that can handle the needs of all divisions regardless of complexity. The product that is a single line item with minimal customer install and support issues is managed exactly the same way that a highly complex product with numerous subproduct definition requirements, major integration issues, long-term installation challenges, and customer support of almost nonstop handholding.

It is this tendency to force the entire company to utilize a single group of tools that often creates major friction with the product divisions. This is no different from the product group deploying new product features that meet the needs of just a few (or perhaps just one) major customer even as these new features unduly complicate the entire product and drive up the cost of deploying the product. Thus, the deployment of negative and destructive inventions can occur just as easily from an internal IT department as it can from a product group.

In this day of application programming interfaces (APIs), Web 2.0 interfaces, software-oriented architectures (SOAs), and the myriad of interface protocols like SOAP and XML, it should never be the case that IT deploys a solution that overly complicates the functions to all the divisions. Even if a single, all-encompassing platform is desired, overlay interfaces should be created that simplify the utilization of that product/platform to the groups that do not need all that complexity. In this way, the concept of a "good enough" product can be tailored to each individual division while still maintaining a single core platform.

By delivering a "good enough" platform (even if it is an overlay approach), the transformative value of the platform to each group will remain high since the increased complexity is hidden away. This approach requires a strong architecture team that can steer the IT foundations to minimize the appearance of negative and destructive inventions to the various product groups. Following the mantra of "maintain a 'good enough' product" will help keep the Big Bang Cycle of IT from ever progressing beyond a stable, productive state. Stability!

BOB SHOULD CONSIDER

- How can we break down our IT products and isolate "good enough" product definitions?

- How can we avoid increasing the complexity and cost of a standardized platform to all divisions while still meeting the niche requirements of some divisions?

- Are we utilizing the best development and product delivery practices to maximize our IT platform flexibility while minimizing cost and complexity?

- Do we have a centralized architecture group that can keep our IT offerings on track throughout the divisions?

Seize Control of Push-Me/Pull-You

Although some external competitive feature pressure can force IT to deliver negative inventions, the most likely external push-me/pull-you is cost. It is easy for external providers to claim that they can deliver better functionality at a lower cost, and it is difficult for IT to counter it unless IT has implemented many of the other items discussed here. We all have horror stories of external IT providers failing to deliver what they promised, and they can often make things significantly worse than they were before.

Kill Assumptions

Killing assumptions is critical for an internal IT department. Often, the functional needs are defined in the various divisions. These functional needs are translated by IT personnel into requirements, designs, and implementations. Depending on the skill of the IT designer, it is not uncommon for IT to deliver something that is far more complex and different from what the division wanted. The problem, to a large degree, is assumptions.

When most software designers start talking to consumers about adding new features, the designers will assume that the consumers know what they want. In many ways, the consumers do know. But, the consumers often don't know how to communicate that want/need to the designer in such a way that the designers can easily pick and choose different design approaches to implement the feature. A consumer will say, "I just want you to add these fields to this web page and process the data this way." The designers will go away with that as the implementation solution and will design the changes accordingly.

In contrast, if a consumer had said, "I need to accomplish so and so," the designers could have said, "Oh, we have functionality very similar to that requirement already in place. Here is how we could enhance it and meet your need."

The IT designers should take responsibility to ask the question, "OK, I see what you are asking for. But, in order to implement it fully internally, please explain to us what you are attempting to accomplish." Then the assumptions are eliminated, and the final changes needed to implement the feature will be minimized.

For IT to deliver what its consumers really need and not what they say they want, IT must take responsibility for eliminating assumptions throughout the requirements, design, and development process. This will ensure that a consumer's transformative value remains high and that the negative portion of the IT innovation life cycle is avoided.

Assumptions are dangerous for everyone in every circumstance. Eliminating them from all IT relationships will maintain the Big Bang Cycle of IT in the Collapse! mode for centralized IT.

BOB SHOULD CONSIDER

- Does our IT group take responsibility for killing assumptions?
- Do we deliver what the divisions say they need to accomplish or what they say they want us to do?
- Are our designers following architectural definitions laid down by our architecture group?
- Do our development processes force us to continuously eliminate assumptions?

Recognize Your Innovation Life Cycle Stagnation

By maintaining a "good enough" IT product offering with niche features through proper architectural approaches, IT can minimize entrance of its products into the negative areas of the innovation life cycle.

In addition to avoiding increases in complexity that impact all consumers, IT personnel should ensure that the costs to each division reflect the actual requirements of the specific division. It is not acceptable to average the costs of the sales platform across all groups when one group requires significantly more complex features than another group.

Although the features requested by one group may be added to the base product, the price of that feature should be zero to the groups that do not make use of the feature. This will maintain the transformative value balance across all consumers.

When the price of a product is generalized to all consumers in spite of the costs being placed by a few niche consumers, the transformative value for the majority of consumers will fall. In the case of IT, this destruction of transformative value through increased complexity or rising costs will shift the Big Bang Cycle of IT toward stage 5, Bang!

BOB SHOULD CONSIDER

- Has our IT group entered into negative invention territory within the product groups?
- Do we balance platform costs to each division based on functional complexity?

Figuratively Commoditize Your Product

I have seen many "wars" within large companies between IT and the product groups. Invariably, IT loses. To counter this result, I have worked with IT departments to figuratively commoditize the products that IT delivers. Through this figurative commoditization, the IT group has been able to isolate the key functions that make up a "good enough" product from the functions that constitute feature enhancements for niche customers. This allows the IT group to reset the transformative value to each group based on that group's utilization of features and based on ongoing product complexity, maintenance, and enhancement issues.

Figurative commoditization in the IT space will also allow the IT department to determine whether its current implementation is overly complex or can be replaced with a different "good enough" product. Through the black-boxing of features into business functions, the IT department can map the business requirements of the existing platform to competitive solutions and choose the best platform for the entire company.

Figurative commoditization is also an excellent tool for the IT architecture group to determine how to evolve existing platforms into newer delivery methods that will simplify the platform and reduce the costs to specific groups.

The Big Bang Cycle of IT can be forced to remain in stage 1 by utilizing figurative commoditization to constantly reevaluate the transformative value of the product/platform to each individual division. Collapse!

Isolate Intellectual Property

In my experience, most attempts to replace existing complex IT platforms will fail because of the tremendous amounts of proprietary business logic that are buried throughout the platform and that are poorly understood or even unidentified as such. It is this intermingling of proprietary business logic with a "good enough" product that will, over time, dramatically increase the complexity of the product and the costs of new product innovation.

In some cases, the proprietary business logic is real intellectual property. In other cases, it can just be customizations added for niche consumers needs. It is critical that the IT department isolate what is really intellectual property and what is not. We discussed several approaches to intellectual property isolation in Chapter 7.

By isolating intellectual property, the IT organization can determine whether the IP can be applied in other platforms or product niches. It also gives IT a definition of differentiators between the internal product and external competitive offerings. Failure to isolate IP can limit the ability to maintain a centralized IT approach and accelerate the Big Bang Cycle of IT toward step 5, Bang!

10

Innovate to Dominate

Companies whose products are dominant in the market do not necessarily stay dominant. In fact, it is all too common for the dominant player to experience the full negative aspects of the innovation life cycle. As their products commoditize, the companies need to innovate in order to maintain or grow their positions and/or shift to a different market.

Markets and Commoditization

A product is said to be a commodity when, although there is a demand for the product, any differentiation between different versions of the product from different manufacturers have largely vanished. This type of definition works great when we are discussing a simple product, such as milk or lead. But, for more complex products and markets, commoditization can appear vastly different.

There are probably an infinite variety of ways to distinguish one type of market from another. When I look at markets and their impact on innovation, I break the markets down into three categories:

- **Flat markets:** These are the markets for "natural" commodities.

- **Compressing markets:** These are markets where there is initially a high- and a low-end version of the product, but over time, the prices, quality, and features converge.

- **Diverse markets:** These are markets where there will likely always be a high- and a low-end version of the product, as purchasers at the high end require custom features that the low end will not require.

Flat markets are controlled largely by simple supply and demand. Milk is the perfect example. If farmers produce less milk, the price tends to rise. If they produce more milk, the price tends to fall. The quality is generally regulated and consistent across all manufacturers. Flat markets are commoditized from day one and remain that way moving forward.

Compressing markets fall more into the range of consumer-based products. PCs are a great example. Initially, the price differential between a low-end PC and a high-end PC was very large. Over time, high-end features have become more universally available so that the feature differences between high-end and low-end have shrunk, along with the price differential and quality differences. It is no longer the inclusion or exclusion of a feature that drives differentiation but rather the size/volume of the feature such as more or less disk space or more or less memory.

In a compressing market, the dominant company will likely sell products throughout the entire market to both the low end and the high end. This is because the concept of a "good enough" product at the low end is relatively easily expanded into a "good enough" product at the high end. The overlap between the two products is high, and the price differential is not so great that the dominant company will focus exclusively on the high end.

Diverse markets generally have a baseline product and a much more powerful/capable upper-tier product. Even if feature differences shrink, there is always a difference of the requirements or expectations of low-end purchasers versus high-end purchasers. Automobiles are a good example. Even though you can buy excellent cars at reasonable prices, there will always be a market for high-end luxury or performance cars.

Software is another example of a diverse market. The feature set required by the low-end user can be substantially different from the high-end user's requirements. The high-end expanded feature set will likely never completely shift downward because the low-end user simply has no use for the expanded features regardless of the cost.

Because of the large differences in features between low-end and high-end products as well as potentially large price differentials, it is very common for the dominant company within a diverse market to continuously attempt to shift its products more and more into the high-end space and to abandon the low-end, lower-margin customers.

As we shall see, a company that wants to remain dominant within a market through innovation has to react differently depending on the type of market it is selling into.

Leaping from One Market to Another

The dominant company in a compressing market will often attempt to shift its intellectual property into different markets. This is exhibited today by PC manufacturers that are aggressively entering the enterprise server market. These manufacturers are attempting to exit the commoditizing PC market and enter a newer market where the differential between low end and high end is still large.

However, it can be seen that aggressive competition has arisen in the server market even at the high end. Like the PC market, the enterprise-class server market is also a compressing market. Over time the server market will compress into a commoditized state, and manufacturers will need to leap into yet another market to find the margins they need to sustain their growth.

In anticipation of the compression of the enterprise server market, many of the same companies are now entering the "solutions" market, again because of the high price differentials between low-end and high-end solutions and services. Unlike the PC and server markets, the services and solutions markets are far more likely to remain diverse markets with large price differentials between low-end and high-end customers.

We will discuss in a later chapter the challenges that these companies will face evolving from products to solutions. A company's required reactions to changes within a compressing market are completely different from the reactions required to changes within a diverse market. Unfortunately, the ability to leap from one market to another is not as readily available within a diverse market.

Sometimes Leading Makes You the First to Fail

A dominant company in a diverse market is very likely to continuously attempt to move upward from the low-end customer to the high-end customer and to abandon the low-end customer in the process. Generally, the revenue opportunities are substantially larger at the high end.

Unfortunately, being the dominant company at the high end of a diverse market can create a staggering array of problems, some of which we have discussed already. As the company attempts to increase revenues at the high end, the tendency is to continue to expand features and increase prices accordingly. Since there is little more high end to penetrate, the dominant company invariably meets and exceeds the "good enough" product even for the high-end customer. Eventually, the company shifts into the negative end of the innovation life cycle and starts delivering negative and destructive inventions, forcing down the transformative value to the customer.

The dominant company in a diverse market will often create the following problems:

- Overly complicated product that has been expanded to meet the specific needs of the high-end customer

- No longer able to deliver a "good enough" product to the low-end customer

- Product is hard to decompose and potentially impossible to shift intellectual property to alternative markets

- Competitors rising up from the low-end customers who the company had previously abandoned

- Competitive products that are less expensive and have not undergone negative or destructive incremental invention

In many ways, the dominant company within a diverse market will, through the decisions that it makes, drive its product toward a limited market (small number of high-end customers) and therefore toward no longer meeting the needs of the overall market.

For purposes of this chapter, we will focus our examples and the rest of the discussion on a dominant software company that is selling products within a diverse market.

> **BOB SHOULD CONSIDER**
>
> - Have we abandoned the low-end customers within our market?
> - Could the potential competitors selling to the low-end customers become our biggest competitors in the future?
> - Are we forcing ourselves to be dependent on an increasingly smaller number of customers and killing our product with negative inventions at the same time?

Isolate the Drivers of the Consumer's Transformative Value

If you were to evaluate the transformative value for each of the competing products within a diverse market, you would likely find that the dominant company has shifted furthest away from a "good enough" product. This is because the dominant company has likely secured the largest accounts, and in order to keep these customers happy and to justify ever-increasing prices, the company has expanded the product definition beyond what the average customer needs or wants.

In the case of a software company, each of the largest customers is likely asking for customizations to better match the product to the customer's business model. The software company will then attempt to resell these additional feature customizations to all the other large customers in the market in the next major release. Unfortunately, not all the customers will view these "enhancements" as features that they want to pay extra for. But, in order to get the various bug fixes and baseline enhancements, they are forced to upgrade and to pay the increased cost or to abandon the software product altogether.

This "do it once and sell it to all the customers" model is very common. Almost every software company follows some form of model similar to this. In the process of implementing such a model, the software company quickly severs its relationship with the low-end customer who is unwilling to pay premium prices for features that it does not need.

The software company needs to return to its roots and map out the transformative values for both the low-end and high-end customers. What makes the product viable for each submarket? It is critical to take actions to drive your product's transformative value back up. This will likely require very hard decisions. Once a product has reached the negative end of the innovation life cycle, the only sure way to regain transformative value quickly is to cut the price. In other words, you must stop looking at the product's high-end customers as the company's only growth generators. By following other areas of the innovation checklist, you can start to shift into new markets or even utilize your dominant position with the low-end customers to garnish new revenue streams within the same market.

Once you isolate the drivers of your customer's transformative value, take action as soon as possible, even if the actions are internally painful. Otherwise, your competition will utilize your current loss of transformative value to unseat you as the dominant market player.

Fully Understand Your Product Delivery Chain

If you are the dominant market player with a damaged transformative value, you can actually reorient your product road maps and intellectual property to penetrate other markets without negatively impacting your original product's transformative value further. Your customers already consider your product as overpriced and overly complex. By taking fast action to cut prices, you can gain a reprieve and use the time to examine other areas such as your product delivery chain for potential innovation opportunities.

Your product delivery chain is probably filled with processes, procedures, and capabilities that your competitors find difficult to compete against. One example is that instead of slashing your product support staff in response to the drop in revenues, you could utilize your employee's expertise to partner with other providers that service your high-end customers. This would allow you to expand into blended services and become more integral to your customers and create new partnerships. Your partners can benefit from your dominant market position and from the stability of your product delivery chain.

Examine your product delivery chain and determine whether your skills and capabilities can be repurposed to increase your company's overall transformative value. Don't limit your view to the transformative value of your product. Your company has an overall transformative value of which your product is a component. So, before you look at portions of the product delivery chain as costs that need to be slashed, examine the potential of repurposing them, even if that repurposing is on a pure cost basis with no contribution to the bottom line.

Align the Different Viewpoints Within Your Company

This is one of the few areas where I recommend the "Everyone in the company should innovate" philosophy. By drawing on all of the players within the product delivery chain, you can often find amazing ways to innovate new products and markets. However, be sure that the executive team is fully on board and that there is a clear definition of the target goals.

Target goals for a dominant player in negative innovation territory are normally easy to define but hard to realize. This is because the goals are almost always based on revenue targets and not on increasing the company's transformative value. Trying to increase revenues in the short term under the existing product offering model is almost certain to fail since the transformative value is low. Goals must be defined that are oriented toward recovering the transformative value, and all groups within the product delivery chain must align behind the goals.

I have never seen a large dominant company succeed in increasing its product's falling transformative value without the senior executive forcing the changes into place. Although I do not think a turnaround executive is necessarily required, the chief executive must unequivocally dictate that each group must come up with ways to repurpose personnel or intellectual property in such a way as to increase the transformative value of both the product and the company. Alternatively, if such repurposing is not possible or practical, then the organization must look for a partner to perform the same functions.

Isolate Pain Points in the Product Delivery Chain

If you are the dominant player in the market, you should have some power over each of the suppliers and partners within the product delivery chain. When your product's transformative value has dropped significantly, you no longer have anything to lose by threatening to replace your partners. Pain points should be crushed as quickly as possible by either replacing or "blackboxing" the offenders. This is especially true because you can decelerate or eliminate delivery of new features, since you have already entered the negative end of the innovation life cycle.

In this age of standardized interfaces, it is possible to black-box almost any hardware or software component in a product and then layer new functionality on top. I have worked with companies that have traditionally had one-year feature delivery windows largely because of the turnaround time of their partners. When we reworked the product delivery chain to include more black-boxing and outsourcing, we could often accelerate the new feature delivery time to less than four months, reduce costs, and still create a good clean product. In fact, the new product delivery chain often corrected a great many product issues, and the decreased turnaround time and costs often boosted the product's transformative value.

Reenergize the Transformative Value Chain

Let's face it, we all attempt to get as much as we can for the lowest price possible. Unfortunately, this goal often destroys the revenue value of your product to your suppliers. Their margins become so thin that they don't really care if you keep buying from them.

Please note, I am not advocating that you ask your suppliers if they will please raise their prices. What I am advocating is that you make sure your suppliers have a reason to help you be innovative. This may require you to purchase more components from one supplier at a slightly higher overall cost. You want your suppliers to have a vested interest in helping you reinvigorate your product's transformative value. This vested interest is created by shifting your focus back from the customer and onto the entire transformative value chain. All suppliers should be partners . . . and not in name only. Partners share the pain and the rewards of a balanced transformative value chain.

Define a "Good Enough" Product

At one time you probably had a "good enough" product that would meet the needs of the vast majority of the market. Although the niche customers may have been willing to pay a premium, the shift into negative and destructive invention has probably greatly suppressed that willingness.

You can use the following ways to identify and deliver a "good enough" product:

- Look at your successful competitors in the low-end customer space. They probably have a great example of a "good enough" product that can cover the breadth of the market.

- Rebrand your existing high-end product, and sell it at a lower cost with some disabled functionality. In other words, hide the fact that they are the same underlying product while benefiting from the common product branding.

- Decompose your product, black-box the "good enough" portions, and then layer on niche features. In other words, rearchitect your product offerings. Don't make it the best rearchitecting ever; just tear it apart and deliver a "good enough" product. There will be time for doing it the best possible way later.

- Utilize screen-scraping or other technologies to create simplified overlays of your product. In simpler terms, hide the monster under the covers.

This is one of the most difficult things I have seen companies attempt. They are so committed to their traditional delivery cycles and on "building for the future" that they can't react quickly. I have found that playing the role of a hardcore purchaser normally solves the problem. In other words, do the following:

- Tell the team they have three days to come back and describe how they can decompose the existing product into a "good enough" product offering. Don't put limitations on time or money.

- When they return with a multimillion dollar, multiyear development effort, tell them you need something that can be delivered much faster. Tell them it doesn't have to be perfect; it just has to get to market fast. Give them another three days.

- When they return, ask them what they can eliminate to further shorten the time frame. Give them another two days.

By giving the team an open field to examine in the beginning, they looked for the absolute best way to do it. In the process, they should have mapped out the key steps to decomposing the product. By telling them that they have to be much more aggressive on the time, they will return with trade-offs. The trade-offs are what you probably don't need in a "good enough" product anyway. Finally, telling them they can eliminate still further gets them to thinking about the bare bones of the product. The bare bones of the dominant product are probably right on target for a "good enough" product for the rest of the market.

Never give the team more than three days. I have found that people will kill themselves to be creative and come up with a great solution when they are reporting to the CEO in three days. The urgency is felt, and the team members see it as an opportunity to show off their skills. Tell them to drop everything except extreme mission-critical items and get it done in three days. Besides, if you give them a week or two, most of the team won't start working on it for half the time allotted, and they don't seem to be half as creative. Don't ask me why the answers are better with a short fuse. I am not a psychologist. I just know it works.

Seize Control of Push-Me/Pull-You

You have the dominant product. If you are responding to push-me/pull-you pressures from competitors, then you need to back off and relax for a while. Don't let your customers or revenue needs pressure you into it either. Push-me/pull-you, as we discussed earlier, is one of the most destructive product evolution methods in existence. Your product will become a mass of tightly woven noodles in no time.

As the dominant player, though, your product may have some subset of features that are "cool to have" beyond a typical "good enough" implementation. By deploying your "good enough" product with a few of these extra features, you will become the leader in the push-me/pull-you game. Force your competition to respond to you, not the other way around.

It is even more critical to stop playing push-me/pull-you during the late stages of the innovation life cycle. Although delivering some product features to your high-end customer may temporarily slow the decline of your transformative value, these features are unlikely to increase the transformative value. Your competitors already have delivered the feature, and your transformative value is low. Adjust the transformative value in other ways, such as price decreases or blended services, while you rearchitect your product into a "good enough" product with niche feature add-ons. Then you can control the push-me/pull-you, increase your transformative value, and force your competitors to respond to you.

Kill Assumptions

As the dominant company with a falling transformative value, you are probably delivering an increasing level of negative and destructive inventions. To a large degree, you are being forced down the incremental path and away from disruptive innovations by assumptions. These assumptions can be related to many areas, including the following:

- You have assumed the breadth of your market incorrectly or have not taken into consideration the shifts and changes that have occurred within the market.

- You have assumed that your larger customers are dependent on your product for their success. Although in some cases this may be true, most of the time it is not. Your customers could just as easily black-box the functionality of your product, modify their business processes, and replace your product with a "good enough" product at a lower cost.

- You have assumed that your existing product road map is the best road map. In reality, your road map may be focused on revenues rather than transformative value, which can be misleading. This is often particularly true in the negative side of the innovation life cycle.

- You have assumed that your resources that are dedicated to a particular product cannot be easily repurposed to create new products and markets. Again, the inhibitor is probably based on revenue goals of the existing product rather than the capabilities of your company's resources.

Assumptions are the killers of innovation and lock companies into inside-the-box thinking. You are the dominant competitor, so kill all assumptions!

Recognize Your Innovation Life Cycle Stagnation

If you are in negative invention territory on the innovation life cycle, stop trying to add more features, and start trying to disrupt the innovation life cycle. By recognizing where you are within the innovation life cycle, you can respond accordingly. Otherwise, you will continue to expect to generate growth from areas that are doomed to fail.

Break your market into pieces, and define a new innovation life cycle for each market. View each product offering, even though they are largely similar, as completely different products. If you have managed to create a baseline "good enough" product, then it should be treated as having its own innovation life cycle. Then all of the niche features should be layered on the "good enough" product to create other innovation life cycles.

Having multiple innovation life cycles that target specific market segments will allow you to recognize when any one of your product offerings is heading into negative innovation territory, and you can respond optimally.

Figuratively Commoditize Your Product

If you haven't figuratively commoditized your product, then you are very likely to drive completely through the innovation life cycle with no hopes of disrupting it or creating alternative product offerings for new markets.

Through figurative commoditization, you can see what functional intellectual property you have available. In many cases, especially in the hardware and software industries, a product may consist of more than 50% functional features that can be easily used to penetrate a new market. Some Fortune 500 companies have figuratively decomposed their IT products and found an extremely large overlap between each product.

Until you complete a figurative commoditization of your products, you cannot determine what other markets you could shift your intellectual property investments into.

Isolate Intellectual Property

Isolating and defining what your intellectual property is may seem quite difficult. In reality, it can be done, at least at a high level, very quickly. The first step is to look at your product's functionally and decide the key features that distinguish your product from your competitor's products. OK, that was really the only step. At a high level, those key distinguishing features are reflections of your intellectual property. You can often use those functional definitions to explore alternative products and markets.

To explore deeper, take each of the key distinguishing features, and ask your team to describe how they function internally in ten steps or less. More than likely one or more of those steps will be intellectual property that can be shifted to other products and markets. Combinations of steps can also be key intellectual property.

To explore even deeper, ask developers to list the top five pieces of code in the product that they think are "cool" and why. Almost always at least one of those cool pieces of code is intellectual property. And in many cases all five will be intellectual property, especially in large systems.

Map Intellectual Property to New Markets

Once you have determined what your intellectual property is, you need to determine how it can be used to build new products and new markets. This is one of the points where everyone in the whole company can become an innovator. Publish the list of key intellectual property concepts to everyone in the company. Keep it high-level for the nontechnical staff, but include some backup details for everyone. Then offer an incentive, such as long-term profit sharing, to anyone who comes up with a viable alternative product or market, based on your intellectual property. Be sure they understand that it is OK if you have to create new intellectual property to flesh out the product.

Normally, I frown on the "Make everyone in the company an innovator" philosophy. But, if the foundational IP has been defined for them, then it is a very different situation.

Oh, and I would be prepared for more than one winner.

Create Disruptive Innovations

Stop being afraid of disruptive innovations. Most large dominant companies focus so intensely on their existing products and markets that they rarely "risk" attempting to create a new disruptive innovation. By following the other items on this innovation checklist, you can largely eliminate the risk factors. But, the tendency to question the viability of the new product and market will still be there in the management team. You must be willing to at least evaluate potential new products sufficiently to understand the transformative value of the products before you reject them. It should be obvious by now that a product with a high transformative value in a large market is like inventing the smartphone. You have to be willing to fund some level of analysis; otherwise, you are destined to disappear as a dominant competitor when you reach the end of the innovation life cycle.

11

Innovate to Conquer

Conquering a dominant opponent does not mean duplicating the opponent's products or capabilities. To conquer, you must create a product that steals the transformative value of the dominant opponent and then not follow the same negative paths of the incumbent dominant company.

Business Life Cycles Revisited

As we discussed in Chapter 4, "Business Life Cycles," there are potentially thousands of different ways to view the activities surrounding a product, market, or company. We covered a baseline of business life cycles that map directly to the innovation life cycle, as depicted in Figure 11.1.

To conquer an existing dominant competitor, you must understand where that competitor is within the various business life cycles. Throughout this discussion, we will talk as if you are competing against one competitor. But, the approach can, and should, be used to evaluate all competitors in the market.

For the purposes of conquering a dominant competitor, you must understand the positioning of your competitor. To that end, the innovation checklist has been changed slightly in order to direct attention at the competitor more than at your own company and product. You would, of course, want to review Chapter 10 to ensure that you are not following the same path as your dominant competitor. Dominance can be achieved without a company falling into the negative territories of the business life cycles, but normal business practices and decision making will naturally push a company into those areas.

Throughout this chapter we will be utilizing your competitor's experience as your training ground. To conquer them, emulate the best of them, and replace their worst with your best.

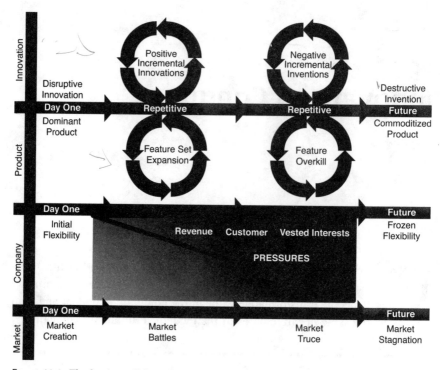

FIGURE 11.1   The business life cycles

Isolate the Drivers of the Consumer's Transformative Value

We discussed earlier that you can use all the aspects of the innovation checklist both to your company's advantage and to your competitor's disadvantage. In the case of attempting to steal market share from a dominant competitor, the checklist can prove extremely valuable. While working with many companies, I have seen that the tendency is to focus on understanding the customer and the market, with very little focus on the competitor. In a market where a dominant competitor already exists, it is extremely valuable to understand the *competition* and not just the competitor's product offerings.

If your company is *not* the dominant company, then you have two basic choices when it comes to competitive strategy:

- **Compete directly**: Attack the dominant company on its home turf with a feature-to-feature battle.

- **Compete indirectly:** Attack the dominant company by reducing its product's transformative value.

The first approach, direct competition, is almost always the way that companies do battle. They attack through ever-increasing features, slashing costs, expanded customer support, and so on. The company's goal is to appear to be better than the competitor in all aspects. The results of such an approach are very similar to the old model of trench warfare. Each side moves the battle line back and forth a mile or less, with casualties and costs piling up everywhere.

The second approach, indirect competition, is far more subtle. It is based on changing customers' perception of the products available in the space. This can be done by evolving the needs or the perceived value of the product to the customer.

The first step is to segment the market and decide how those market segments are served by existing products, including your own. Are there niche markets that are poorly served? Are most competitors pursuing the same set of customers?

The second step is to determine which market segments have the most customer churn. These segments are potentially the ripest for a new dominant competitor. Don't fall victim to the old question, Is the churn the result of the quality of the customer? The low "quality of the customer" is a fatal assumption and is very seldom the real cause of customer churn. In reality, the churn could be caused by the features-to-cost balance that forces consumers to reevaluate the product they are using. In addition, the company providing the products in high-churn segments almost always creates a well-defined point of reevaluation for consumers. An example would be the two-year contracts in the cell phone market. These effectively force consumers to reevaluate their service provider every two years.

The third step is to determine the average revenue per customer in each market segment. This should include the potential for up-selling additional products and services.

The fourth step is to select market segments that maximize your potential and minimize the potential of your competitors. This should be the area where you attempt to maximize your product's transformative value.

I have seen many sales teams spend a tremendous amount of time and money responding to requests for proposals (RFPs) and requests for information (RFIs) from potential customers in market segments that have extremely low churn rates and very high competition. Because the probability of winning a contract or product sale in such a segment is extremely low, the new competitor will often lower the prices of its products in an attempt to appear more competitive than the incumbent. Although this may increase your product's transformative value, it rarely lowers the transformative value of your competitor's product. Churn is created most frequently when the competitor's transformative value falls below customers' acceptable levels, not just when your transformative value rises. Cutting prices in an attempt to get the contract will most likely set you up for failure or be used by customers to force the incumbent competitor to cut its costs. Either way you will lose while your competitor may win.

Over time the dominant competitor will most likely damage its own product's transformative value. You should position yourself to take advantage of this. As we discussed in Chapter 4 concerning the market life cycle, use the market truce period to prepare to conquer your competitor. Don't continue trying to fight a face-to-face battle. Otherwise, your product's transformative value will fall right alongside that of the dominant competitor.

Fully Understand Your Competitor's Product Delivery Chain

By reviewing your competitor's product offering, you can often determine how the product is delivered. Is part of the product manufactured by a third party? Does the product require a lot of customization to satisfy the larger, most desirable customers? Is there a long supply chain requirement to deliver the dominant competitor's product?

Since you are attempting to compete in the same space, there is probably overlap between your product delivery chain and the product delivery chain of the dominant competitor. Map out this information so that you understand where the overlaps exist and where the distinctions exist.

The overlaps can reflect four states of comparison between your product delivery chain and that of your competitor:

- They're mutually efficient.
- They're mutually inefficient.
- Yours is more efficient.
- Yours is less efficient.

By categorizing the overlaps in this way, you can quickly visualize the areas that can benefit your product delivery chain the most.

If the overlap is mutually efficient, then you would not want to consider this intellectual property or a competitive advantage. Initially, you can ignore such areas. But, later you should review whether completely different approaches can make your approach more efficient than the competitor's.

If the overlap is mutually inefficient, then you have identified a prime opportunity for impacting your product delivery chain, transformative value chain, and product transformative value in very positive ways. You may be able to accomplish these positive factors and decrease costs at the same time.

If your approach within the overlap is more efficient, then you have identified a piece of intellectual property or competitive advantage that can be used to maximize the potential for this product and the potential for new product innovations.

If your approach within the overlap is less efficient, then you have identified a key shortcoming in your product delivery chain, and your competitor has provided you with a sample of how it can be improved.

Utilizing these overlap distinctions, you can either evolve toward your competitor, isolate your intellectual property, develop new and more efficient alternatives, or do any combination of these.

Many disruptive innovations come from changes within a product brought on by new suppliers and channel partners that exist within the product delivery chain. Utilize your competitor's product delivery chain to drive your company's identification of potentially disruptive innovations.

Align the Different Viewpoints Within Companies

We have talked a good deal about how the differing viewpoints within a company can force the company down paths that appear to be the best financially but that are not optimal either for innovation or for maintaining the transformative value of the product.

Ask yourself, Do you have insight into the pressures within your competitor? Is anyone on your product development team, sales team, or management team a former employee of the competition? Can you identify internal pressures within your competitors through discussions with independent consultants who work with all competitive products, including yours?

Most companies are, frankly, terrified of this topic. They are so worried about being seen to steal product technology from a competitor that they rarely talk to new employees about previous employers. Obviously, you never want anyone to violate a nondisclosure agreement or an employee agreement.

However, the goal here is to understand the mind-set of the competitor. What markets are they most focused in? Are customers generally happy with new releases? Are most product development efforts focused on existing customers? The focus should be on trends, not specific details. The trends are normally personal opinion, whereas details would be proprietary information.

By gathering as much personal experience information as possible, you can then correlate that with the product offerings, news releases, product release cycles, and many other areas that are publicly available to determine the probable mind-set of the management team inside the competitor.

Isolate Pain Points in Your Competitor's Product Delivery Chain

You probably have pain points within your product delivery chain: a supplier that is very slow to respond to new requests or a channel partner that acts more like a competitor than like a partner. If you have these types of pain points, then it is almost a certainty that the dominant competitor in the market has similar pain points.

If you discovered overlaps within your and your main competitor's product delivery life cycles, then you can likely identify whether you have similar pain points. It is these pain points that can be used as distinct advantages for innovation. The innovation could be reflected in time to market, costs of products, feature simplification, and so on.

The pain points of your competitor are also highly valuable for increasing your product's transformative value while decreasing your competitor's product's transformative value. Remember, the goal is to accomplish both your own increase and your competitor's decrease in transformative value, not just one or the other.

Finding the pain points of the competitor can be fairly straightforward. In this day and age of virtually unlimited access to information, it is very easy to determine who is partnering with whom and who is supplying to whom. Each player in the competitor's product delivery chain is most likely utilizing that relationship publicly to attempt to garnish more market share within its own markets. So, searching through news releases and other Internet-based information will provide a wealth of information on how companies are working together. By tracking these partnerships, you can normally see how one partner is impacting the other partner.

The slower a competitor responds to a new feature in the market from a different competitor is also a good sign of pain points within its product delivery chain. You can value your own company's ability to deliver the feature and then compare that to the dominant competitor. Then, depending on the type of feature, you can determine where the likely pain point (if there is one) probably resides. Does it exist within the internal development team? Does it indicate that the base product architecture is less flexible? Is the pain point with an external supplier? Is it an integration problem between internal and external suppliers?

We will discuss shortly how you can further utilize the push-me/pull-you of new feature delivery to intentionally force the competition to reveal its product delivery chain pain points.

Reenergize the Transformative Value Chain

The dominant competitor has probably done the most to streamline the product delivery chain and has also probably compressed the transformative value chain the most. This will often be reflected in a slowdown in how its partners deliver new product features. If the revenue value within the relationship has fallen, then the partner will be much less inclined to move quickly when creating and delivering new features.

This compression of the transformative value chain has the negative effect of starting to drive down the product's transformative value in the eyes of the consumer. It is this reflective property of transformative value that you can utilize to your company's benefit. By definition, the competitor is forcing down its own transformative value through negative incremental invention and destructive inventions. The competitor is very unlikely to reenergize its transformative value chain because that often implies increased revenue opportunities for partners and suppliers and a resulting cost increase for the competitor.

Over time, the dominant competitor is likely to become effectively locked in with particular partners and suppliers. Each new feature it gets from the supplier increases this locking pressure and reduces its opportunities to shift from one supplier/partner to another.

These areas of locked-in high dependence within the competitor's transformative value chain are your perfect opportunity to find lower costs and accelerated product innovation within your own transformative value chain.

By reenergizing areas that overlap, you can effectively improve your innovation life cycle and utilize this to conquer the competitor.

Define a "Good Enough" Product

As we touched on in Chapter 10, sometimes being the leader is not a good thing. This is especially true when it comes to defining and deploying a "good enough" product. Since you are not the dominant competitor, you have ideally not fully entered the negative side of the innovation life cycle. This should make your product more flexible and less expensive to evolve to suit niche markets.

I won't use explicit examples of software systems that have gone far beyond "good enough" and are now so complex and cumbersome that virtually every customer talks down about the systems. I am sure many of you have your own examples. And many of us have casually tried to visualize how to fix these behemoth products.

Take that same visualization experience and look at your competitor's product. If you ran your competitor's product development group, how would you downsize the product into a "good enough" product? And what market segment would you target that "good enough" product toward?

Many initiatives to rebuild these behemoth systems into more usable platforms have failed. They have become so interwoven with special features to meet niche market needs that decomposing them into "good enough" products may no longer be practical.

Delivering a "good enough" product, even to the high-end customers, is often viewed as highly market disruptive. These products can be cheaper to acquire, can be easier to use and deploy, and can provide more flexibility for the customer to evolve their own business.

By reviewing your competitor's ability to deliver a "good enough" product, you can determine how long it would take the competitor to respond to your own delivery of a "good enough" product. By delivering a "good enough" product in stages to particular market segments and later focusing on the high-end customer, you can often delay the reaction of the dominant competitor until the very last minute.

Seize Control of Push-Me/Pull-You

When you can be in control of it, push-me/pull-you is one of the few opportunities you have to force an entire industry to run in directions that potentially have little or no value to the competitors or to the customers. The trick is to be in control.

The first step is to never, ever look at your competitor's new product release from a feature point of view. The features mean absolutely nothing if they don't also provide a positive change in the consumer's transformative value for the product. So, look to how the new release changes the transformative value to the consumer. Will the transformative value be likely to increase? Did the features make the product more complex? Will this result in a decrease in transformative value? If the transformative value remains the same, then the competitor spent a lot of money delivering new features that add no long-term value.

The second step is to determine whether your competitor is delivering niche features or market features. Will the features increase the transformative value to your competitor's market niche, or is the competitor changing the definition of what a "good enough" product is for the entire market? Is the competitor responding to specific feature requests from high-end customers you currently do not have?

If the new features deliver a positive change in the transformative value of the competitor's product and they are targeted at a market segment in which you are competing, then you may need to respond. However, do not respond by simply implementing the same feature set. This is the normal response from the development team: "We can easily implement that same feature in our next release."

Instead, look at why the transformative value is expected to rise. Will it increase the customer's perceived value of the product? If so, how does the perceived value change? Is it a time or money issue? Does your product's transformative value consist of the same perceived values as the competitor's transformative value?

In addition to responding to your competitor's actions, you can also force the competitor to respond as well. Since the competitor is unlikely to do a review of how your new features are impacting the customer's transformative value, then they can only assume that the impact will be positive. There is that *assume* word again—only this time it is your competitor who is assuming.

If your product falls into a category that allows a lot of incremental invention, then you should try throwing in some new features that are inexpensive to deploy, that do not corrupt the "good enough" product, and that deliver positive value to your customers. These could be a small support menu in a software product or a monitoring tool for a hardware deployment.

Even if you don't have the flexibility to deploy "test" features to watch your competitors, you should be watching your competitor's responses to all of your feature releases. Each reaction from your competitor will tell you more and more about its internal processes, product delivery chain, transformative value chain, and pain points. Push-me/pull-you analysis will tell you how hard it is for your competitor to evolve its product.

Kill Assumptions

Assumptions are rampant everywhere. If you create assumptions on purpose, then some assumptions can be good. For instance, by getting your competition to believe that you are focusing on a different market segment when you offer a less powerful, "good enough" product, you can utilize that assumption to surprise them when you become a high-end competitor.

When competing with the dominant competitor with high-end customers, you must avoid having customers assume that you have a very similar product but are not as capable as the dominant company. This assumption forces customers to lower the transformative value of your product.

One of the best ways of stomping out this "similar but not equal" product comparison is to get away from doing just feature comparisons. Always remember: *Features do not necessarily imply transformative value!*

Unfortunately, most organizations provide information to customers through data sheets, competitive matrices, and many other documents that are all just feature-based. Then customer lists, partner lists, and other information are layered on in an attempt to influence the customer. Rarely does the potential customer receive an explanation of why this product should have a higher transformative value than the competitor's product.

Food advertisements are some of the best examples of extolling the transformative value of a product rather than the features of the product. When was the last time you saw a candy bar commercial that was comparing the ingredient list to a competitor's product? Everything is convenience, cost, flavor, and other areas directly impacting the perceived value of the product. Comparisons are done through "taste tests" or customer reviews, not through comparisons of basic ingredients or data sheet equivalents.

Some food advertisements focus on having less fat content. Although this is probably good for the dieting market segment, almost everyone equates "less fat" with "less flavor." Be aware, therefore, that it can be tricky focusing on transformative value for a specific, narrow market segment, because such focused statements can damage the transformative value to customers in other market segments.

In this day and age of audio, video, and multimedia presentations, it is far simpler to deliver a virtual demonstration of the transformative value of a product and its competitive products. In a few minutes, a good video can demonstrate how a product meets all the perceived values of a consumer market and in effect demand that consumers recognize a higher transformative value for the product.

Many smartphone advertisements are great examples. They show how touch-enabled features allow for simplification and how that simplification provides access to a large number of capabilities that can impact money and time. So, even without a full understanding of how to make a smartphone work, consumers will likely assign a high transformative value to them. These smartphone commercials are directly oriented at the "I" rather than the "we" of the target market by making it appear that you can meet your individual needs simply and quickly.

Recognize Innovation Life Cycle Stagnation

The dominant competitor in many cases will already have entered the negative territories of the innovation life cycle. By recognizing the competitor's innovation stagnation, your company can innovate in completely new and distinct directions by utilizing the dominant competitor's innovation attempts as clues.

It is sad to say, but you can almost depend on the dominant competitor to remain in negative invention territory and to fail to innovate its way out of this stagnation. But, the more external pressures that are brought to bear, the more likely the dominant competitor is going to attempt to aggressively lash out through cost cutting or new innovation.

From your point of view, as a competitor seeking to conquer, you might consider actually decreasing competition with the dominant competitor until you are optimally prepared to conquer them. Backing off the pressure on its product's transformative value will likely delay any response the competitor would otherwise have. In other words, let your competitor's product's transformative value continue to fall while you create the best "good enough" replacement product. Obviously, there are many circumstances where such a strategy will not work: markets with many aggressive competitors, markets with minimal churn opportunities, and so on. To determine whether a delay strategy is appropriate, be sure to fully evaluate not only the dominant competitor but other direct competitors, potential market entrants, customers, and your own internal capabilities.

Figuratively Commoditize Products

By figuratively commoditizing your competitor's products, as we discussed in Chapter 7, "The Innovation Checklist," you can often predict where your competitor will attempt to push its product moving forward. This will allow you to prepare for a shift in competitive positioning and to maximize your own product's capabilities to counter such a product shift.

In addition, figurative commoditization of the dominant competitor's product will give you the foundations for positive incremental innovation of your own product to compete for the high-end consumer through acquisition or partnerships. This functional breakdown can guide you to filling your own product feature holes.

Isolate Intellectual Property

Intellectual property can be viewed as being foundational inventions. You have your intellectual property, and your competitors have their intellectual property. The company that succeeds in evolving that intellectual property in the optimal manner will very likely become the dominant competitor, both within the existing market and within potentially new markets.

Isolating intellectual property in a competitive product can be extremely difficult. The first place to examine is what patents the competitor has applied for and been granted. These patents can guide your product team in understanding what your competitors consider to be their intellectual property. This guidance can then be extrapolated into what markets the competitors are most likely to apply their intellectual property.

Map Intellectual Property to New Markets

You can map your competitor's intellectual property to new niches within the current market as well as to other potential markets. Reviewing these potential market changes can provide tremendous innovation insight into how to evolve your own products and intellectual property.

Remember, the company that creates a new market has a definite advantage (if the company exercises it) for a limited period of time to dominate the new market and to gain from disruptive innovation aftershocks. If you can utilize an analysis of your competitor's intellectual property as seeds for new product innovation within your own company, you can be significantly ahead of the game within the current and new markets.

Create Disruptive Innovations

Don't follow your competitor in the push-me/pull-you model. Minimize risk, minimize cost, and maximize market penetration by fostering innovation through analysis of your competitor's innovation attempts. By utilizing all the information that the innovation checklist allows you to derive concerning your competitors and markets, you should be able to develop disruptive innovations instead of incremental innovations.

New product features are reflections of potentially long and expensive research and development efforts. By understanding how those features impact the transformative value in the market, you can bypass a great deal of the R&D and pick and choose which competitive features can be deployed to optimally increase the transformative value of your product.

Try new, potentially disruptive innovations on niche market segments first. These segments will be much easier to satisfy since the target transformative value can be much more highly refined. In other words, create a "good enough" disruptive product that fits a niche rather than the entire market. If the product fails to become a runaway hit, it will still demonstrate ways to innovate new potentially disruptive features that can be used throughout the market.

12

Innovate to Disrupt

D id you ever look at a market and say "Wow, I could do that so much better!" even if you are not currently a competitor with a product in that market? Well, there are ways to enter the market without having to take on the big guys who are already heavy hitters within the market. And even better yet, the big guys will show you how to succeed and disrupt their own market position.

Market Reverse Engineering

I am sure many of you have tried to start a company or develop a product idea. Although it may have appeared to be straightforward when you came up with the original idea, the implementation is often a long, painful, expensive, and risky process. Writing business plans, market analyses, product descriptions, competitive comparisons, cash flows, and all the other business paperwork needed to get funding and to justify developing a product that doesn't exist yet can take months and months.

It would be much simpler if the market was already there, the product descriptions were pretty much finalized, and the penetration potential of the product was already well documented. The only real problem would be demonstrating that you can compete effectively against an incumbent competitor who has an existing product and customer base. Ouch. That can be a very large problem!

But, the nice thing about almost any market is that there are underserved and unserved consumers who would likely benefit from a "good enough" version of those existing products. And the amazing thing is that the existing competitors will guide you away from all the problems they have already encountered . . . for free!

Why don't the existing competitors penetrate the underserved and unserved market segments? There can be many different reasons depending on the particular product and market, but here are some general guidelines:

- The product pricing is outside the range of the market segment.

- The current cost structure of the product delivery chain is too high.

- The product complexity exceeds what the market segment requires.

- The existing sales/delivery models do not work well in the market segment.

- The customer support requirements in the market segment are too high.

- The average revenue per customer is too low.

The list could go on and on, but this is a good sample list of reasons that existing competitors do not penetrate particular market segments. In some cases, these untapped market segments make up a huge percentage of the customer population. For instance, large enterprise resource planning (ERP) software companies focus on medium to large enterprise customers. And yet, there is a largely untapped market in the small to medium business (SMB) customer space. Many SMBs could benefit from the capabilities of a decent, limited-function ERP package, especially if the package had an almost zero cost of entry, very fast deployment, and limited commitment requirements. Cloud computing could easily make the penetration of ERP solutions into the SMB space much easier.

As we shall see, the current market competitors are continuously providing a highly detailed view of how to effectively compete against them.

Isolate the Drivers of the Consumer's Transformative Value

We talked briefly earlier about luxury items as well as perceived value. To me, a $200,000 automobile is an extreme luxury item that has very little transformative value. To some wealthier individuals, the transformative value of such a vehicle could be quite high. To someone making minimum wage, the transformative value would be negative because just maintaining the vehicle would likely exceed their means. So, perception by the individual consumer segment is critical to defining the type of product that will have positive transformative value within that segment.

To enter an existing market as a new competitor, the easiest approach is to penetrate those untapped market segments where the transformative value of existing products is close to zero. By examining the current market competitors, it should be a fairly easy and quick process to determine who is not being served and why.

As we discussed in Chapter 2, however, it is critical that you accurately define the full market. Each market segment should then be defined based on the drivers of the transformative value within each segment. In the case of automobiles, there are many segments based on functional usage by the consumer. Is the consumer single or married? Are there children or other dependents? Do they need to transport materials, people, or both? Are they interested mainly in style or function or both? Does gasoline mileage matter? How critical is it for the automobile to have a very high reliability rate?

I know a guy who has five different models of a particular luxury car manufacturer. He doesn't need five cars. He just loves them. He loves the customer service he gets when one of them needs a repair. He is single, has no children, travels a great deal on business, and is rarely home. When he is home, he wants to drive around in a nice car. He doesn't care if one is less reliable than another. In spite of issues that would make most of us sell a car, he still loves them because while the dealer is repairing one of them, he is sitting at the dealership having fun with other luxury car owners. It is one of his major social groups.

Here are some of the major steps you should follow to garnish valuable understanding about the transformative value of the product within the market:

- Define the attributes that will distinguish one type of consumer from another, such as married or single.

- Define the market segments within the target market based on these attributes.

- Define what the perceived value of the consumers within each market segment would be for a version of the product. Don't restrict the definition of the product. Make the product definition flexible for now.

- Define the size of each market segment.

- Determine what competitors sell into each of the market segments.

- Ask the question, "Why does this competitor sell into this market segment?"

- Ask the question, "Why does this competitor *not* sell into this market segment?"

- Correlate the product definitions required to enter each of the poorly served or unserved market segments. Create a single "good enough" product definition.

- Determine the transformative value of the "good enough" product relative to each of the market segments.

- Estimate the cost of deploying the "good enough" product based on analysis of existing competitive products.

- Estimate the average revenue per customer for each market segment.

- Adjust the product definition to maximize transformative value within underserved market segments.

- Attack and disrupt.

This is a simplified list to demonstrate how you can utilize the existing competitor's products and its transformative values to understand market dynamics, isolate drivers of a customer's perceived value, define competitive pressures within each market segment, and address many other critical areas.

Define a "Good Enough" Product

It can be extremely challenging to separate the technology view of a product from the business view of the same product. Many products fail because they are based too much on technology and not enough on the business/consumer view. The reverse situation can also exist where the product doesn't utilize technology effectively enough to meet the consumer-defined perceived values.

The really nice thing about penetrating an existing market is that almost all of the research and development of what is a "good enough" product has already been done. And, depending on the size of the market, there are experts running around all over the place who will tell you exactly what a "good enough" product looks like. I am speaking of the many system integration companies, independent consultants, and consumers who are fluent in multiple product offerings from multiple competitors. For the price of a short consulting assignment, they will all tell you the pros and cons of each of the major competitors and will guide you directly at what constitutes a "good enough" product definition.

The independent consultants are often the most valuable because their entire livelihood is often based on filling in the gaps that the current competitors are not filling. These consultants are providing much of the product evolutionary force that is needed by the high-end customers.

In a similar fashion, the system integrators are often able to flesh out an understanding of each of the market segments and how the competitive products fall short, meet, or exceed the requirements of each segment. Their livelihood is often based on servicing the niche markets.

At least initially, don't get too creative about what a "good enough" product is. Rely on the existing competitors to guide you. This will help create the foundational "good enough" product that you can then target through layered features at each market niche. Minimize your initial risks by avoiding attempts at truly disruptive innovations. The time for disruption will come, but first, focus on controlling underserved and unserved market segments with a well-understood "good enough" product.

Fully Understand the Product Delivery Chains

To disrupt the market that is largely controlled by incumbent competitors, you must control costs and features to maximize product penetration and maximize consumer transformative value.

Many existing products are built on legacy technologies, and the product delivery chains are reflections of that legacy. Apple is one of the few companies that will almost completely reinvent a product from one generation to the next. The Apple iPod shuffle is a great example. The external appearance varies so greatly from one product generation to the next that it is difficult to categorize them as the same product. Yet, functionally they are extremely similar. Apple is constantly evolving each of its product lines to take advantage of newer technologies and better component pricing, size, energy consumption, and so on.

But, most companies, especially companies selling software products, do not have the flexibility to evolve at the speed that Apple evolves the iPod. The suppliers to these software companies, be they internal or external, appear to be unable to deliver highly diverse and quickly evolving innovations in a short period of time. And Apple products are largely focused at all consumers, not just a high-end customer segment like those pursued by many software and services companies. So, other than colors, shapes, or different storage capacities, an Apple product line will have a fairly consistent feature set.

The product delivery chain of a product that has evolved over time can be long, convoluted, and definitely not optimal. It is much easier to create an efficient and cost-minimizing product delivery chain by starting with a "good enough" product definition based on existing market penetration.

Here are some high-level steps that will allow you to benefit from the product delivery chains of your competitors:

1. Review and understand the product delivery chains of each of the current market competitors.

2. Define a potential product delivery chain for your "good enough" product.

3. Compare and contrast your product delivery chain with that of your competitors.

Isolate Pain Points in the Product Delivery Chain

By monitoring the product release schedules and the types of changes within the new versions of a product, you can often deduce where problems exist within the product delivery chain. This is especially true if you understand the current technologies that are available to build a "good enough" product from scratch that utilizes the latest and greatest technologies. When a competitor fails to utilize the latest and greatest in a new release, there is a reason. It could be legacy architecture of the product, supplier commitments, manufacturing difficulties, or any number of other aspects of the product delivery chain limiting its product evolution.

By identifying these pain points, you can often identify potential disruptive innovations. Remember that many disruptive innovations are based on inventions that are largely combinations of other foundational and functional inventions. If you can deliver a "good enough" product that utilizes the latest and greatest technologies, then you can immediately displace the "good enough" version from competitors who have been unable to deliver the same technologies.

Seize Control of Push-Me/Pull-You

Watching competitors pound away at each other in the push-me/pull-you circle can be extremely entertaining and informative. If you can obtain publicly available release notes that describe the features of prior and current releases, you can track the evolution of a competitor's product in a fairly straightforward manner. You can detect the following concerning product architecture and evolution:

- Where the competitor considers its technical "sweet spot"

- Where the competitor considers its product to be "weak"

- How the competitor is interpreting the transformative value of its customers and how the product must change to meet those customers' needs

So, if new features are gathered around particular functional areas, then there are a few likely reasons for this:

- The competitor is attempting to strengthen its sweet spot.

- The competitor is attempting to strengthen a weak spot.

- The competitor is enhancing certain areas because of contractual requirements from customers.

As a competitor delivers more and more features, you can quickly deduce many things about how the competitor is viewing the market as a whole. Based on your market segmentation, you can tell whether the competitor is moving toward any of the market segments that are currently underserved or unserved. You can even tell whether the competitor is moving away from a market segment into which it is currently selling.

Recognize Their Innovation Life Cycle Stagnation

To fully understand how your competitors are functioning and where they are in the innovation life cycle, you need to dig further into those publicly available release notes you acquired for the push-me/pull-you analysis. The key to understanding a competitor's position within the innovation life cycle is to document how the new features in each release are perceived by the customer.

Utilizing those independent consultants we discussed earlier, you can quickly determine whether new features were perceived as positive or negative and how much impact they had on the existing customer base. A trend of delivering new features that have little or no positive impact on the customer's transformative value for the product is a clear indication that the company is in the negative incremental invention or destructive invention stages of the innovation life cycle.

If you can determine that particular features were delivered to satisfy the needs of one or more high-end customers and if these features were generally perceived as not positive by other customers, then you can assign these features to the destructive invention category.

It is not critical that you fully understand the innovation life cycle position of your competitor. But, the more you know, the more likely you are to make the correct decision in a push-me/pull-you confrontation, and the more likely you are to avoid negative invention territory.

Isolate Intellectual Property

Your competitors may own one or more key pieces of intellectual property that they consider to be foundational to their products' success. In many cases, there are alternative solutions to the same problem that do not violate patents or other mechanisms competitors use to protect that intellectual property.

In fact, if you can isolate what competitors consider to be their technical advantage, then you have found an extremely valuable key into how they are likely to respond in future product releases. I like to call this the **guru factor**. Virtually all product teams have one or more technical leaders who have been around for a long time. They are involved in every aspect of the evolution of the product. And, unfortunately, they can be the greatest impediment to new innovation. Their entire involvement with the product, following the initial product release, has most likely been one of incremental innovation. The guru carries all of the accumulated assumptions around as foundational knowledge.

By isolating the competitor's "technical sweet spot," you have probably identified the foundational assumptions of the guru within the product development team. You can then create an alternative product path for your "good enough" product that bypasses this technical sweet spot and allows much more flexibility within your product than within the competitor's product. You can use this knowledge to basically force the competitor deeper and deeper into negative and destructive invention territory.

Isolating the competitor's intellectual property is by no means simple and requires a great deal of review and discussion. Your product team should be heavily involved in this process from the very beginning.

Map Intellectual Property to New Markets

How will your competitor respond to your entrance into the market? If you first penetrate the underserved and unserved market segments, then the competitor's response will likely be very minimal. But, while you are penetrating these segments, you should be actively aligning your "good enough" product to penetrate your competitor's market segments. Once you attack your competitor on its home turf, your competitor will most likely ignore you until you steal several of their largest customers. Remember, your competitor's tendency is to remain on an incremental track with its product.

Your competitors could, however, recognize the need to shift into new markets and could begin to isolate their intellectual property and attempt to innovate new products. Much of their energy in pursuing this will come from the competitive pressure you are creating.

Prior to entering the home-turf market segments of your competitors, you should have already mapped out how they might shift into new markets. You should also have reached a decision on whether you will precede them into these markets. Don't follow the normal innovation life cycle unless this is the only market you want to participate in. Take advantage of your newer product delivery chain, and enter alternative markets early. In other words, follow the Apple example. Define your advantage, maintain that advantage, and utilize that advantage across as many markets as possible. Your competition will still most likely be weighed down by a legacy product delivery chain as well as a huge pile of assumptions. For any alternative markets your competitors enter, you, almost by default, should have a distinct advantage over them.

Create Disruptive Innovations

Disruptive innovations can be caused by as little as a change in packaging or a change in product size or product convenience. The underlying functions don't have to change all that much. The Sony Discman was a portable music player. By shifting from hard media (CD) to soft media (memory) and by drastically reducing the size, the iPod became a resounding success. The underlying function of a portable music player remained the same. The market was already well defined, but now new market segments could be penetrated in addition to the already served segments.

While you are creating a competitive product for the market your competitors have defined so well, look for the small changes in your "good enough" product that would be perceived as highly disruptive. Most likely these have some impact on cost, complexity, or convenience. Your definitions for the transformative values for each market segment should be able to tell you the common thread that you can improve upon to change your "good enough" product into a market-disrupting product.

13

Organizational Structure: Products to Solutions

Unfortunately, there is no innovation magic wand. You can't simply buy the right wand and wave it over an existing company, product, or market and . . . *voila!* . . . have an innovation. Many companies in the hardware, software, and communication industries are trying to evolve themselves from product manufacturers/providers into solution providers. They wave the management, structure, and budget wands, but all too often fail to deliver new innovative solutions. Why do they so often fail?

Products versus Solutions

Back in the long-ago days of the sixties through the nineties, companies such as IBM, Wang, Amdahl, and others would sell a combination of three primary things:

- Hardware

- Operating systems and support systems

- Business applications

In general, these were wrapped together with a lot of custom development designed to match the specific business requirements of the large customer. This customization was the superglue that locked the customer onto your hardware and operating system. Look around at almost any large, older enterprise, and you will discover that it is still maintaining and running applications on hardware that should have been buried long ago.

As time passed, the hardware got smaller and cheaper. Hardware and operating systems began to commoditize. I remember trying to justify to a customer in the seventies why the identical software functionality running on a mainframe should cost 1,000 times more than the same functionality on a PC. Hardware and operating systems largely shifted to stand alone from business applications and fell out of the superglue customer retention equation.

Developers began to create very powerful business applications that were hardware and operating system agnostic. This drastically expanded in the nineties with the advent of powerful networks and the concept of distributed processing. The justification for unique business applications started to vanish. The higher-level business application functions, except in very specialized areas, began to lose their superglue capabilities.

With the advent of high-speed networking and the demand for real-time data processing, the need to integrate diverse applications became more and more critical. Where two systems previously ran on completely independent systems, now there was a need to integrate the systems together either through batch update mechanisms or through real-time integration. This integration requirement quickly became the new superglue of customer retention.

But, custom development of the integrated applications also created a great deal of risk to the enterprise customer. Delivery schedules for new features would often slip no matter how critical they were to daily operations. And the integrated application superglue became extremely expensive over time. Adding custom innovations could often be almost impossible.

With the arrival of large-scale outsourcing of IT development and support, enterprise customers no longer wanted the risk of expensive software development or long innovation lead times, and they desperately wanted to dissolve all the existing superglue. It is at this point that the hardware and software companies began to realize that they had to deliver business solutions, not just hardware features and software functionality.

Business solutions have to deliver a very high integrated transformative value to the business customer. I use the phrase *integrated transformative value* meaning that the transformative value of the solution is a reflection of many diverse impacts on the company. Otherwise, it would still be called a product with a much simpler-to-define transformative value.

BOB SHOULD CONSIDER

- As we are visualizing our solutions versus our products, are we reevaluating the customer's transformative value?

> • Are we targeting the solutions to maximize the impact on the customer's business? Or are we trying to maximize the number of our products that are part of our solution, regardless of the impact on the customer's business and the resulting integrated transformative value?

Stages of Organizational Change

IBM, a company that routinely shows up in lists of most admired companies, has largely shifted from the world's largest computer manufacturer to one of the world's largest hardware/software solution delivery companies. This has been a long transition but one that IBM has executed superbly through acquisitions, restructuring, and creative management. Many speak of following the "IBM model" toward becoming a solution company. But, how do companies try to reach the goal of matching the IBM model?

Shifting from a product company to a solution company is not a simple act of defining a new group of products that are labeled as solutions. However, that is often the first thing companies will attempt. Nor is it as simple as reorganizing existing product groups so that they have more of a solution orientation. The changes needed to shift from products to solutions impact every single aspect of the company from purchasing to sales as well as all the research, development, and manufacturing groups in between.

I have watched many companies pursue this shift over the past ten years, and invariably they all follow a similar evolutionary route of organizational change (that is, unless the company declares bankruptcy and makes an extremely drastic shift to survive). Each of these stages of organizational change has a different impact on the company's ability to innovate new products, attract new customers, and penetrate new markets.

I summarize this evolutionary organizational change into the following categories, which we will discuss in more detail later in this chapter:

- **Product company:** Existing product delivery infrastructure

- **Rebranding:** Calling a product a solution with some feature shifts

- **Executive mandate:** Executive push of existing product groups

- **Overlay organization:** Overlay organization to align the product groups

- **Solution group:** Stand-alone solution group

- **Solution company:** Solution delivery nirvana

Over the past decade or so I have watched the traditional phone companies change their branding from "phone" to "telecom" to "service" and now to "solution" companies. I chuckled because inside they were still the same companies. They didn't want to remain "bit haulers" because that model has commoditized. And yet, they are still built around the legacy audio conversation and per-minute billing. In an era when there should be no distinction between having an audio conversation, participating in a video conference, watching a movie, or roaming the Internet, the carriers are often still segmenting the consumer's activities into minutes or messages or kilobytes. These are not solutions; they are products. It is critical that you eliminate or evolve the foundational assumptions that may be forcing your company to remain in the past.

BOB SHOULD CONSIDER

- What stage of organizational change are we currently in?
- Are we limiting our ability to evolve into a solutions company because of foundational assumptions about what a solution is?
- Do we need to offer solutions that are potentially radically, and therefore disruptively, different from our existing products?

Product Company

Product groups evolve to become extremely good at delivering products. They optimize the product delivery chain and focus all internal processes on delivering the best product possible. This includes how research and development is performed, how marketing is managed, how the sales force is compensated, how the customer is supported, and a thousand other factors that fit in with maximizing the quality of the product.

Being a product company has its own positives and negatives when it comes to innovation. On the positive side, incremental innovations can be extremely well targeted to the specific markets for the products. On the negative side, targeting specific markets over an extended period of time will create "the box" that will make it almost impossible for the product team to break out and deliver disruptive innovations.

Eventually, unless there is some kind of monopoly in play, all product companies will see their products reach a state of commoditization on the negative side of the innovation life cycle. It is often at this point that the company begins to try to expand its role beyond simple products and attempt to rebrand itself as a solutions company. It would be far more optimal for a company to recognize that it has entered the negative side of the innovation life cycle and to begin the shift from a product-based company to a combination of products and solutions.

BOB SHOULD CONSIDER

- Are we a product company?
- Are our products at risk of becoming, or have they already become, commoditized?
- Do we need to break our product developers out of the box that we have created? Or do we need to create a new solution group that doesn't exist within the same box?

Rebranding

Rebranding probably makes it sound like the company is trying to pull the wool over the customer's eyes. In reality, companies often don't see the extreme difference that should exist between a product and a solution. The company feels that adding new features or delivering product simplifications will change the product into a solution.

But, the key is to watch for changes in the transformative value. If the new "solution" does not substantially increase the breadth of the transformative value through larger impacts on the customer's business, then the product changes are merely incremental product changes and not solutions. In fact, the new "solution" is most likely a continuation of delivering negative incremental inventions that will force the product further toward commoditization.

Rebranding is the least expensive, least risky, and least successful approach to shifting from a product company toward a solution company. Rebranding is also easy to identify and easy to avoid. If the effort needed to deliver the new solution versus the old product consists mostly of marketing and sales activities with a slight change in product development road maps, then you are probably rebranding. You will waste time, waste money, and further endanger your company's survival.

Rebranding avoids the hardest issue in evolving from a product to a solution company: organizational and process changes. Without these changes, it is extremely unlikely that a product company can reverse the drive toward the commoditization of its products. Solutions by definition must have a broader, more integrated transformative value. This can occur only by the blending of multiple products and/or services into a single solution delivery. This blending can normally not occur within a product group–structured company.

Bob Should Consider

- Are we fooling ourselves and wasting time and money by expecting a rebranding effort to change us from a product to a solution company?
- Did our new solution initiative create large changes in our product road maps?
- What processes will we have to change in order to foster a solution orientation within our company?
- Have we compared our new solution transformative value to our product/service transformative values?
- How can we maximize the integrated transformative value of our new solutions?

Executive Mandate

When the rebranding effort fails, the company leadership will often blame it on the abilities of the management teams within the product groups. Although this may be partly true, the response of the leadership is often to throw down the gauntlet and mandate that product organizations work together to create a more integrated solution. At this stage, the company is starting to realize that a solution requires a blending of products and services.

Mandates rarely work. The employees and the management definitely understand that solutions would be much more likely to guarantee the survival of the company than separate commoditized products. So, mandating that "everyone pursue one goal" oversimplifies the problem and demonstrates that perhaps the wrong leadership team is in place to accomplish the product-to-solution evolution.

If we were to examine the history of a large product-based company, we would undoubtedly see that each employee, manager, and executive has been trained, selected, and promoted because of their success at delivering products. All of the corporate measurements are designed to reinforce this product orientation. Annual reviews and raises are targeted within the product group. Budgets and management teams are aligned to product groups. Sales forces are compensated on product sales, with commissions often tilted toward particular product groups that are the most profitable for the company.

Here is an example: I was working with a large product-based company that was under an executive mandate to deliver solutions to the enterprise customers. When I spoke to individual sales teams about selling the proposed solutions, they privately told me that they would not sell the solution because it was too risky for them. Their "bread and butter" came from product sales, and they did not want to risk a good relationship with the customer by delivering an untested solution. They said, "Let someone else sell it to their customer first." Since I had never worked in sales at that time, I was floored. Now that I understand the way sales force commissions are often defined, I sympathize with the sales force completely.

Almost everything that executive mandates accomplish is normally negative. Management teams and employees are often judged on criteria that the corporate processes and organizational structure do not allow them to meet. They are expected to meet their existing product budget and sales projections while working with other product groups to create solutions for which they are not rewarded.

From an innovation point of view, the executive mandate can be particularly stifling. Product groups will often attempt to align their product road maps into a pseudosolution road map. But, without a separate management team with the power and budget to drive the solution road map forward, much of this effort will only deliver increased product complexity, slow down product feature delivery, aggravate large customers, and further damage the transformative value of each of the products.

BOB SHOULD CONSIDER

- We have very talented employees and management. But have we considered the fact that they are the best product people around and not necessarily the best solution people?

- If we continue to sell our product, then we will still need our talented product people. Doesn't this mean that we need new solution people right away?

continues

- Have we mandated to our company that everyone deliver solutions without changing any of the processes and procedures that we use to measure the success of our employees?
- By mandating, are we creating chaos in our product groups and stifling the very innovation that we were hoping to increase?

Overlay Organization

When the executive mandate fails, the leadership team will often decide that what is needed is an overlay organization that has responsibility for creating the new solutions. This organization will be funded by the product groups, has a small dedicated staff with additional staff that is "matrixed" over from each of the product groups, and will focus on solution road maps, marketing, and sales support.

I equate the overlay organization to the captain of a boat who does not directly have power over the boat, the crew, or the mission. The captain may have all the best intentions, but each of the crew members will pursue activities that are best for that particular crew member. The captain has to borrow resources continuously, and the direction the boat is headed may be changed by the owners of the boat, that is, the executive leadership team, at any time. An overlay organization is often captain in name only.

In an overlay organization, the individual product road maps are rarely controlled by the overlay organization. The overlay leader must ask the product groups to embed new features into the product road map. These are often at the bottom of the product group's list of critical features. Even if these negatives are not true and the leader of the overlay organization has true power to impact product road maps, the likelihood of success is still very small—not because of a failure in the overlay organization but because of the small number of people within the company who are designated as "solution" people. Remember all those employees and managers who are perfect for delivering products? Well, in the case of an overlay organization, they are still in place, and they are still doing what they have been trained, selected, and promoted to do, which is to deliver products.

In my opinion, leading an overlay organization has got to be one of the most frustrating and career-limiting roles around. The likelihood of success is almost always close to the zero mark. After a year or two at the most (and often much less), the product groups will aggressively question why they are required to fund and staff an organization that is not delivering solutions but only a package of products. And the product groups will have a great deal of evidence of the failure of the overlay organization, such as slipped schedules, confusing road maps, lack of technical leadership that is accepted by the product groups, and much more. Even if the overlay organization is staffed with the best leaders around, they will find it almost impossible to eliminate the foundational assumptions that exist within each product group.

Innovation is once again severely dampened during the overlay organization stage. Road maps are poorly aligned, and yet changes are being made to products in an attempt to fulfill the overlay organization's goals. The leader of the overlay organization is often, at least initially, more politically powerful than the legacy product groups. This power can force product groups to refocus or abandon existing road maps. It is not uncommon for some product areas to completely collapse as funds and staff are drained away to support the activities of the overlay organization.

BOB SHOULD CONSIDER

- Are we robbing the funds and staff of our product groups to implement an overlay solution organization?
- Have we anticipated the negative impacts on current product road maps, sales, and customer satisfaction that will be caused by borrowing resources from the product groups?
- Can we maintain or increase the transformative value of each of our products while, at the same time, deliver an integrated transformative value through a new solution offering?

Solution Group

After the leadership team fires the leader of the overlay organization (this appears to be the normal turn of events), the leadership team will finally determine that the evolution from a product to a solution company can be accomplished only by creating an organization that is designed to develop solutions. If the executive team is smart, they will place the product groups under the solution group. Otherwise, this stage in the organizational evolution will actually be two stages: one with no control over the product groups and eventually one with control. It is critical that the product groups be treated as separate providers within the new solution delivery chain. Yet, unless the product is fully commoditized, the solution group must control the product group's road map.

The solution group stage can be extremely expensive to deploy. There must be a distinct team that is defining, packaging, selling, delivering, and supporting the solution. This team can consist of people taken, not borrowed, from the product groups, but the new team must stand alone. If the product group is still selling a stand-alone product, then the group will need at least some portion of their team to remain intact.

The solution group stage is normally hampered in the beginning by the executive team's unwillingness to fully fund and staff the group. They now understand the need for a separate solution group orientation, but they think that the new solution group management is overestimating the staffing and funding requirements. Although this may be true, it is far more likely that the new management is actually underestimating the costs and staff needs. The expertise often does not exist within a product company, so new hires are critical to success. The duplication of sales and support teams is almost a definite.

When the solution group is staffed and funded correctly, true innovation of new products and markets can often occur. Negative incremental invention within individual product groups will almost immediately cease, and disruptive innovation becomes far more likely.

A huge number of potential approaches and combinations could prove to be successful in attempting to create solution offerings from within a traditionally product-oriented company. For instance, utilizing an overlay solution with an executive mandate and sufficient funding could satisfy the same requirements as a stand-alone solution group. These "solution hybrids" allow different methods of cutting over from a product-only organization to an organization that contains elements of a dedicated solution group while meeting the unique structural, historical, and financial situations of each company.

BOB SHOULD CONSIDER

- Can we bypass all the intervening steps of organizational change and jump directly from a product company to a solution company?
- Are we potentially underfunding or understaffing the new solutions group? Are we just delaying the inevitable and hurting our innovation opportunities and products in the process?

- Have we determined which products should be controlled directly by the solutions group and which need to stand alone?
- How will we measure the success of the solution group? Is it more difficult to measure than that of a product group?
- How will we know whether the apparent failure of the solution group is because of a lack of funding, lack of marketing, lack of sales because of too high a price, or any number of other potential causes?

Solution Company

After a period of success within the solution group, the company will most likely begin to shift in its entirety toward solutions. This often means that existing product groups may be spun off to allow the company's solutions to be built on products currently offered by its competition. The more generic the solutions are relative to the underlying products, the more likely the solutions are to take on a superglue effect. This is especially true when many of the components of the solution delivery chain have become commoditized. The costs of internally developing and maintaining what is otherwise a commoditized product as part of the solution will only decelerate the solution road map and increase solution delivery costs.

Product companies can become solution companies while still having their own in-house product development. The two are not mutually exclusive. The important stage in the conversion of a product company to a solution company is where the innovation of products is driven by the innovation of solutions and not the other way around.

BOB SHOULD CONSIDER

- Have we determined which products we should keep because of their intellectual property and which products should be spun off?
- What new markets can we enter if we decouple our solution offerings from our product offerings?

PART IV
Innovation Deployment

1) patents, trade secrets
2) Time to build, time to market, time for competitor to displace
3) Endurance
4) partners & relationships
5) 15 Secs → invention, innovation,

14

Valuing Innovations

What is an invention or an innovation really worth? We all know where many estimates of projected sales come from. Out of thin air! But, there has got to be some way to understand the true potential of an innovation.

Inventions versus Innovation

Way back in Chapter 1, "Inventions and Innovations," we separated inventions from innovations. This was critical for understanding that you can invent all you want and still not deliver an innovation. And through continuous invention, you can actually damage your existing innovations by decreasing the transformative value of the innovation through increases in complexity and cost and through decreased competitiveness. To summarize, invention does not imply innovation, and too much invention can destroy innovation.

When it comes to valuing an invention or an innovation, the distinction between the two is just as critical. I draw the line this way:

- Invention: An invention is the foundation for one or more innovations and can be valued based on its ability to impact other innovators and innovations.

- Innovation: An innovation is the foundation for one or more markets and can be valued based on its ability to impact the lifestyles of consumers.

You will see in the next chapter how critical it is that you be able to articulate the value of your inventions and innovations when it comes to marketing your company and products to investors, advisors, and consumers.

Valuing Inventions

When you are looking at a company's technology, be it a physical product or a logical process, you need to determine what the foundational inventions are that the company actually owns or controls. You should keep in mind that the ability to package and deliver other people's inventions is also a powerful capability. Many of the largest consumer electronics companies distinguish their products based on their ability to cram more and more functionality into an small, easy-to-use device. The bulk of the embedded technology in these types of devices is largely owned by their suppliers. So, having a great supply chain and product design group can be an extremely powerful invention.

Making the distinction between valuing an invention and valuing an innovation allows us to define valuation factors that are focused on our need for the valuation. In the case of an invention, the valuation is normally oriented toward finding partners, investors, advisors, or even licensors of the technology.

Invention valuation can be broken down in a virtually limitless number of categories, but we will focus on the following primary categories:

- **Patents and other public properties**: How your technologies are protected

- **Trade secrets**: What your "secret sauce" is

- **First to market**: Timing and competitiveness

- **Relationships**: Who is in your network of companies, suppliers, and partners

- **Endurance**: How likely is it that someone else can develop a competing product without violating any of your patents or other legal protections

Patents

First, I am not a patent attorney. I have written a lot of patents, have been granted a lot of patents, and have read a lot of patents. But, I repeat, I am not a patent attorney. For legal advice, please contact a competent legal attorney.

Now that I have done the disclaimer, I can discuss patents openly. Patents are a great tool for protecting technology that can be easily deduced or stolen. Let's say that I produce a watch that has three gears in it that are arranged in a completely new manner that allows the watch to function at extremely accurate time tolerances and with only one-tenth the power requirements.

Would you call this a trade secret and try never to reveal the uniqueness of the gear arrangement? Or would you patent it and make it publicly known?

For me, this astounding new gear arrangement would lead to an immediate patent application. Why? Well, once the new gear invention is released in a watch, the invention is right out in the open for any inquiring mind to reverse-engineer. Opening the back of a watch and looking at the gears takes only a few minutes for even the novice. Without a patent in place, the new gear arrangement will very quickly enter the public domain. This means anyone can copy the gear arrangement and use your invention to compete against you or to enter other markets with no requirement to pay you a royalty.

I look at patents to understand foundational inventions for a company. If the company does not have a patent on its foundational invention, then it had better be able to protect the invention in some other way.

Patents can be a multi-edged sword. The different sharp edges of the sword can do the following:

- Create protection
- Create competition
- Demonstrate infringement
- Open the door for an attack

We already briefly discussed how patents can protect you in the situation where your invention is easily observable. But, how do patents create competition? Many inventive ideas (and innovative ideas for that matter) are really just a matter of perspective. Someone looked at something just a little bit differently than everyone else. You know the situation: "I never looked at it that way before." That's why many innovative products can be traced back to inventions that were largely accidental. The inventors were working on something else, and . . . *bang!* . . . their experiment produced an unexpected result that got them thinking from a different perspective. It is this accidental invention process that creates many executive edicts like "If you aren't failing, then you aren't trying."

When you expose this alternative viewpoint in a patent, you can inadvertently educate your competitors and show them the alternative viewpoint. Now they can sense the same epiphany and work toward finding their own alternative to your invention. So, patents can often create new competition. There are ways, through filing amendments to patent applications, to temporarily delay the granting and publication of a patent. But, new laws in the United States attempt to limit the effectiveness of hiding your technology.

With many companies I work with, I ask them, "How does your competition do this?" My client's idea appears to be something new and inventive, but could the competition already be doing something similar that is already protected by a patent? Unfortunately, a patent search can be a fairly ineffective tool for determining whether your new invention will violate someone else's patent. Subtle wording in patents can make them extremely broad in their coverage. Locating these broad patents, which will often not include any of the key words your patent includes, can be extremely difficult. Even the patent office often does not find them. This is why there are lawsuits that one patent infringes on another. So, will your new patent give your competitor the ammunition needed to come after you for infringement on its patent?

Especially in this day of what were once called **patent trolls** but are now referred to as **nonproducing entities** (NPEs), it is potentially very dangerous to go for a patent on items that can be protected as trade secrets. NPEs look for patents that they can acquire cheaply that have a very broad impact on a particular market. The NPE may be preparing for future product enhancements or may have identified already deployed product features that violate the patent. In both cases, the NPE will approach your company and demand some form of royalty agreement because of your infringement of the NPE's patent. This is a far more common occurrence than is generally known. Many companies settle with NPEs out of court without any publicity. The NPE will then use the new relationship to approach your competitors and demand a similar licensing arrangement. In many cases, the companies follow along.

Even the most innocent display of your product's inventive nature can be fuel for the NPE to become aggressive. I have spoken with numerous NPEs that utilize new release documents and user manuals as a foundation for how a product is evolving. They then project where the company is most likely to evolve its product in the next year or two and begin a fairly exhaustive search for idle patents in that space. In this way, the NPE tries to deduce your product road map and to prepare to attack you in the future. Your patent applications make this extremely easy since most of your development teams are focused on filing patents on short-term, incremental inventions. The NPEs will align to attack your next incremental inventions if they think you have deep pockets and can extract money from you.

When I talk to people at a new start-up company, I expect them to have a plan to protect their inventions either through patents, trade secrets, or perhaps even a physical method, such as encryption or encapsulation. The invention by itself may have little long-term value unless it can be protected. It's much easier to determine the impact of an invention on alternative products and markets if it has an existing patent that has withstood the test of time.

BOB SHOULD CONSIDER

- How much of our intellectual property is protected by patents today?
- Are we patenting based on our future road map or on our current development initiatives?
- Will some of our patent applications provide that "epiphany angle" to our competitors?
- Do we utilize the patent filings of our competitors as analysis data to understand the road map for our competitor's products?
- Is there a way for us to be proactive using the techniques of nonproducing entities for our own intellectual property acquisition and protection?
- What is the risk we face from nonproducing entities?

Trade Secrets

Now, let's take a different example from the new watch gear arrangement discussed previously. Let's say that I produce rocket engines. And I mean the big rocket engines, not the ones for toys. Every time I sell a rocket engine, I can require that my technicians physically attend to and guard the engine. Once the engine is fired, for all practical purposes the engine is destroyed. There is little or no opportunity for a competitor to deduce my inventions through a casual investigation of my product. Depending on how likely a patent on my invention is to give my competition an alternate view epiphany, I may choose to simply hide my invention as a trade secret.

The problem with trade secrets is that their value can be fleeting. Oftentimes, a trade secret is a process of some kind that may be implemented within a software package, in a supply or manufacturing chain, or even in relationship management. Unless these types of inventions can be easily isolated within a product, they will slowly become corrupted over time through normal incremental invention processes. At this point, the inventions protected as a trade secret are rarely able to be used in other applications. They have been integrated and pounded into an existing product or process, and their disruptive potential has been lost.

On the other hand, one type of invention has the potential to be a long-standing secret if closely guarded with appropriate security mechanisms. The most famous example of this is the formula for Coca-Cola, which was invented in the early 20th century and has remained a closely guarded trade secret for about a century. Patenting this formula would have cost Coke billions in past, present, and future profits.

When companies tell me they're going to protect something as a trade secret, I recommend that they still encrypt, encapsulate, and protect it through nondisclosure agreements, product licenses, and so on. In this way, the customer becomes the holder of responsibility for the trade secret. A great many companies' entire business models are to reverse-engineer a product, discover trade secrets, and attempt to lock in ownership of variations of these secrets. Without control on access, trade secrets can become worthless very quickly and can become a potential attack vector for NPEs.

BOB SHOULD CONSIDER

- How are we protecting our trade secrets?
- Can we utilize encryption, encapsulation, or other techniques to try to extend the life of our trade secrets?
- Have our trade secrets become more difficult to quantify and isolate over time?
- Are we prepared to value our trade secrets today, and if we tried, would we come to the valuation we currently anticipate?

First to Market

Getting first to market with a new invention can be the difference between delivering a disruptive innovation, an incremental innovation, or no innovation at all. The risks with a new invention relative to reaching market revolve around three time periods:

- Time to build the product
- Time to dominate the market
- Time for a competitor to displace you in the market

The "time to build the product" is pretty self-explanatory. But, the question you should ask yourself is, "What, exactly, is our product?"

The "time to dominate the market" is a little trickier. Most people assume that if you are the first to market, then you are also dominating the market. Wrong. If a new competitor could enter the market tomorrow and steal your customers, then you are not in a position of dominance. It's kind of like an army conquering a valley but not conquering the surrounding high ground. It is only a matter of time before the army in the valley gets wiped out.

The "competitor displacement" time period is even trickier still. You need to understand your potential consumers' transformative value well enough so that you can aggressively fight back against competitors trying to steal your market position. This is not a battle for feature dominance. This is a battle for transformative value dominance.

I have seen a lot of start-ups with creative new inventions fail because they did not pay attention to these three time periods. These companies had a tendency to be influenced by four of what I call **fairy-tale beliefs**:

- We need to deliver the best product we can.
- No one else has thought of this yet.
- We have the advantage of being first to market.
- If we build, buyers will come.

These four fairy tales become the driving factors in how the start-up company develops its products, partners, markets, and all other aspects of delivering the product to market. Let's discuss the fairy tales and examine the impacts on the three time periods.

One of the problems with engineers (and I consider myself an engineer) is that they don't like anything that can be called a *bug*, *shortcoming*, *flaw*, *missing feature*, and so on. Engineers and technologists in general have a tendency to try to incrementally reinvent an invention before taking it to market. They want to deliver the best product possible. Why? It's because they think they can ignore the first time period, the time needed to build the product. They worry about it, of course. But, they worry more about dominating the market and making it difficult for a competitor to displace. They also have the other three fairy tales to back them up: No one else has thought of it, they will be first to market no matter what, and buyers will flock to their doorstep.

Virtually all truly disruptive innovations are based on inventions that are far from perfect. Within months (sometimes weeks), disruptive products will be enhanced by their producers. And these incremental innovations will strengthen the transformative value of the product. These are the disruptive innovation aftershocks. You should take advantage of these aftershocks to hone your product and optimally position it.

The "no one else has thought of this yet" is one I hear all the time. My response is always, "How do you know?" I go on to ask them whether they are making their product and its potential known widely. Of course they aren't. There could be one, two, or even hundreds of companies working on exactly the same thing. I always assume that there is a competitor pursuing exactly the same invention and innovation as I am. This is the biggest danger to very early start-ups that don't have the funding to lock in their patents or other protections. If you think something should be protected with a patent, you should file a provisional patent as soon as possible. Don't wait for major funding, or you could lose the advantage completely.

The "advantage of being first to market" is similar to "no one else has thought of it." How do you know that a competitor will not come out with a competing product tomorrow? Making any other assumption causes you to lower your paranoia about balancing the three time periods. You need to prepare to be second to market and still win.

The absolutely biggest fairy tale of all, especially when the three time periods mentioned previously are ignored, is the "if we build, buyers will come" fairy tale. I had a venture capitalist (VC) call me last month who had invested part of $40 million over five years into a start-up to build a new technology. The VC called me to ask what markets the technology could be used in. I muted the phone so I wouldn't laugh in his ear. The start-up and all the investors had completely ignored the three time periods. Don't get me wrong; they had built an amazing technology. But, during the five-year development period, all of their target markets had either moved on to different technologies or had commoditized. This is a problem that occurs when you confuse invention with innovation. The start-up had a phenomenal invention. The problem was it was not innovative enough to the target consumer to create a disruption in the market and to garner a high transformative value. You should never, ever confuse inventive with innovative. You should assume that you are wrong about how innovative your product will be and get to market as fast as a balance of the three time periods will allow in order to evolve the product into a true disruption.

"First to market" means very little unless you are balancing the three time periods and avoiding the four fairy tales. When evaluating the value of an invention, you should focus on whether the company is balancing correctly and whether they are trying to write a new fairy tale.

Bob Should Consider

- Are we balancing the build, dominate, and displacement time periods?
- Are we making fairy tale assumptions about the uniqueness of our product, our ability to be first, and our ability to dominate the market?
- Should we be building toward a "good enough" product that will allow us to reach market quickly and then adjust that product with incremental innovations?
- Are we prepared to be the second to market?
- Are we confusing *inventive* with *innovative*?

Relationships and Partners

A lot of start-up companies try to create relationships with the big suppliers and manufacturers. They also try to partner with the most likely companies that can help them penetrate into the product's target market. Such start-ups are viewing the big suppliers and manufacturers as contributors to the valuation of the invention.

Although the relationships and partnerships are critical, they should only be assumed to have a unique, difficult-to-replicate value if the relationship or partnership is based on a transformative value chain that benefits the partner to a degree that cannot be trumped by potential competition.

When examining the value of an invention relative to relationships and partnerships, the key things to consider are the following:

- **Shared intellectual property:** Does the partner have a vested interest in the invention, and is that interest exclusively controlled?

- **Commoditization:** Is the partner supplying a commoditized component or service?

- **Alternatives:** Are there alternative partners with alternative products that will deliver a similar transformative value to the consumer?

When evaluating an invention, I rarely include partnerships and relationships unless they are exclusive, have a defined time frame, and are extremely difficult to replicate.

BOB SHOULD CONSIDER

- Have we examined our relationships and partners from the point of view of a transformative value chain?

- How can we make our relationships more exclusive to protect our balance of the three time periods?

- Are we discounting the ability of our potential competitors to utilize alternative products in their transformative value chains?

Endurance

All technologies are fleeting—or at least they will become accepted and lose that inventive luster. I have grown older with the computer age, and yet I am still amazed by some of the very fundamental technologies that are the foundations of all modern electronics. These technologies have become so commonplace that most people accept them as having "always existed." Or they have been completely displaced by newer technologies. So, the endurance of an invention is critical to understanding its value.

One of my kids, the 15-year-old, was discussing her typing speed at dinner the other night. I described how frustrating some of the old typewriters were. The 10-year-old asked, "What's a typewriter?" And then the 18-year-old chimed in with, "How did you correct mistakes?" I had not realized that my kids younger than 18 had never seen our electronic typewriter in the storage room. I hadn't used it in at least 10 years myself. But, how could a device that at one time was a fundamental component of every office vanish so completely? The stand-alone typewriter simply did not have the transformative value to endure beyond the coming of modern word processing and the PC.

The primary way to determine the endurance of an invention is to categorize it, as we did in Chapter 1, as being either foundational, functional, or product. Unless fully protected by patents or some other mechanism, the endurance of an invention will be lower for a product invention than for a functional invention and lower for a functional invention than for a foundational invention. Products make use of many foundational and functional inventions. Therefore, it is easier to create a competitive, noninfringing product invention than it is to discover a different foundational invention.

Endurance must be balanced with time-to-market considerations to determine the value of an invention. If the invention's uniqueness will not endure long enough for the product to become dominant in the market, then the invention may have a limited value against its competitive inventions.

BOB SHOULD CONSIDER

- Are our inventions foundational, functional, or product?

- Are there ways for us to increase the endurance of our inventions by locking down control of the foundational and functional precursor inventions?

- Are our patents broad enough to protect our product inventions from competitive, potentially noninfringing alternatives?

- Are we placing all of our emphasis on delivering the best product and ignoring the ebbing endurance of our inventions?

Valuing Innovations

Since a great deal of this book has revolved around the concept of a product's transformative value, I am sure you know what I am going to say next. The value of an innovation is based on the stability of and the ability to protect the transformative value of the product. Just because an innovation is doing well in the market does not imply that the product has not already begun to lose its transformative value.

When valuing an innovation, it is critical to determine where the company, market, and product currently stand within the innovation and business life cycles we have discussed. Highly successful products have had their markets collapse very rapidly because of a history of negative incremental invention, gradual decreases in the transformative value, and the sudden introduction of a disruptive innovation. You should not only examine your own position within the life cycles but also examine the position of your competitors.

You should never value an innovation based just on current sales versus competitors in the market. Your competitors may have a smaller share of the market and yet be in a much better position to compete and become dominant within the market.

BOB SHOULD CONSIDER

- Where are we in the innovation life cycle?
- Where are we in the other business life cycles?
- Where are our competitors within the life cycles?
- Are our competitors in a better position within the life cycles than we are?

Multiple Markets

The nice thing about looking at the value of a product from the point of view of its current transformative value is that the transformative value is often an accumulation of multiple factors that impact the consumer's lifestyle. Each of these factors, such as time savings, money savings, and convenience, can be isolated and used to determine whether the innovation's underlying product could be retargeted into alternative markets. For instance, a product that delivers time savings and money savings in one market may also, with minor feature modifications, deliver time savings in a completely different market.

When valuing innovations, I am a firm believer in the "Don't put all your eggs in one basket" motto. In this case, "Don't put all the innovation's value in one market" is more to the point. For many of the reasons we discussed earlier, such as time to market and fairy tales, it is critical to determine whether an innovation has multiple markets that could be attacked either immediately or in the event of a disruption in the existing market.

I consider the "multiple markets" value to be the most critical for any innovation valuation. If the company has innovated themselves into a niche market, even if that niche is large and very profitable, will the company be able to innovate its way into a different niche or a completely different market?

BOB SHOULD CONSIDER

- Have we broken down the transformative value of our innovation?
- How does our innovation impact the lifestyle of our consumers?
- Are there any alternative markets that these lifestyle impacts could be retargeted at?
- Can we innovate our way into a new niche or alternative market?

15

Bringing Innovations to Market

There are probably thousands of great new product ideas thought of each and every day. Many, almost all, of these ideas will never reach a viable market. In this chapter, we will discuss many of the challenges faced by entrepreneurs and start-ups in bringing their ideas to market. For instance, convincing investors that you have the "right stuff" can be extremely challenging. We will also discuss why creating a disruptive innovation is not always a good idea and how to come to market in a "stealth" disruption mode.

Fifteen Seconds to Success

I am sure that virtually all of us have dreamed about having our "15 minutes of fame" as originally opined by Andy Warhol. Sometimes fame is thrust upon people through no action of their own. Sometimes it is the result of a well-defined plan. And sometimes the 15 minutes of fame is the worst 15 minutes of their lives.

When it comes to articulating your invention or innovation to a potential investor, you need to have such an absolute certainty in your initiative that you never waste a single breath. You must know at least the foundational answers to many areas. And if you have to stop to consider how to reply to a question that you should have already considered, you could easily lose any further opportunity with that investor.

Instead of 15 minutes, I believe firmly in a "15 seconds to success" approach. For instance, look at your watch or open your computer clock, and then read the first paragraph in this section. For me, this paragraph takes exactly 15 seconds to read in a clear, well-metered voice—not rushed and not stammering to get my place and gather my thoughts. It's 15 seconds of clean delivery, with four sentences that cover a lot of territory including introducing the possibility of 15 minutes of fame, instilling curiosity about those "thrust upon," mentioning a plan that we all probably want to hear about and follow, and finally the instilling of fear of it all going wrong and a desire to avoid the possibly horrible outcomes.

Being able to articulate in 15 seconds why someone should give you more than the time of day is critical. I know that many of you are thinking "Sure, 15 seconds, never gonna use it." Well, until you discover how valuable mastering that 15-second delivery is, I agree, you will never use it.

I have used my 15-second "elevator speeches" many times. I have actually bumped into a friend on an elevator, who introduced me to someone I wanted to talk to more at a later time. I had only 15 seconds to convince this new acquaintance that we should meet . . . *bang!* . . . 15 seconds of delivery. I have crossed a street and encountered someone that I needed to talk to right in the middle of the street. We were going different directions, but I wanted to follow up with them later and . . . *bang!* . . . 15 seconds. I have grabbed a high-level exec at a conference knowing the person was rushing out to catch a plane. I didn't want to delay them, but I may never have had the opportunity to talk with them again, so . . . *bang!* . . . 15 seconds. Once you master the 15-second delivery and see its value, you start using it all the time where previously you would never have even attempted a conversation.

But, the possibility exists that you will never use your 15-second speeches. Even that doesn't matter. The important thing is that you become an expert at whatever invention or innovation you are selling to the investor. That's because, make no mistakes, you *are* selling, and they get very tired of being sold to by people who don't know what they are selling. They get phone calls, e-mails, and letters by the thousands. They have to decide which to spend some extra time on and which to throw away. *Bang!* . . . 15 seconds.

When people are scanning books on a shelf in a store or the library, they are very quickly looking for interesting content for further consideration . . . *bang!* . . . 15 seconds.

In this modern world of instantaneous communications, texting, digital downloads, and all the other ways in which we are constantly bombarded by information, we are making high-speed evaluations of what to discard, what to consider now, and what to act upon later . . . *bang!* . . . 15 seconds. Our entire business world now competes using a 15-second shot clock!

Preparing and understanding the other areas discussed in this chapter will give you the foundations for your 15-second speech. Prepare it. Practice it. Use it.

BOB SHOULD CONSIDER

- Can we articulate our invention/innovation, market potential, and other key aspects of our start-up in 15 seconds?

- How many opportunities to network with potential partners, funders, and customers have we missed because of the lack of a 15-second speech?

- Telemarketers, salespeople in stores, and even door-to-door salespeople all seem to operate on a 15-second sales pitch. Why are we any different?

- Can we take the 15-second speech and use it aggressively in social media?

- Once we nail down the 15-second pitch, what next?

Time to Think Like a Banker?

Most people who create a start-up company are technologists, marketing executives, or specialists of one form or fashion. Even if they categorize themselves as businesspeople, they are specialists in a particular industry or function or management style. Something makes them good at what they do and caused them to identify a potential invention/innovation that they felt strong enough about to create a company to develop and sell it. I deal a lot with technologists in the computer, telecom, or personal device markets who are running or want to run a start-up.

Unfortunately, for us technologists and specialists, we have a tendency to try to sell the "coolness" of what we have invented. We tend to look at the people we meet, potential investors and advisors, as our peers. We are so excited about our invention that we try to convince them to be excited by explaining all the coolness of our invention. That approach works well when you really are talking to a peer. But, in most cases, venture capitalists, angel investors, and corporate investors are not our peers. They are bankers. And we want their money. And they want to make more money. Money is the key—not cool (at least most of the time).

If you walked in to your local branch bank and sat down with a loan officer to get a car loan, would you start talking about how cool the car is in order to convince them to give you the money? Unless the banker is your brother, you are not going to get the loan.

Or would you try to convince the banker that their money would be well spent on a car worth more than the loan, that the car will remain insured at all times, and that you are capable of repaying the loan with interest? Now you are thinking like a banker.

When it comes to funding a start-up, you have to convince the investor that you actually need the money. Unless it is the best, most highly sought after investment opportunity on the planet, the investor is very gun shy about giving you money for the product that you then use to go buy that cool new car we talked about.

You need a 15-second speech that covers how much you need and why.

For instance, you need something like this: "We have developed a new method of distributing audio content directly into MP3 players without a physical connection. We need $2 million for the first round for nine months to finish the prototype, finish market trials with key consumer product manufacturers, lock down our intellectual property, and hire staff. This is a potential $2 billion market."

Once again, the previous paragraph is a 15-second delivery for me. It covers the invention (new method of distributing audio content into MP3 players), innovation (no physical connection), money requirements ($2 million), time frame to market (nine months), investment round (first), road map (prototype, trials, manufacturing, patents, staff), reference to unique intellectual property, and market potential ($2 billion).

Once you have delivered this 15-second sales pitch, you have given the investor a great deal of information so that they can decide what to do next such as one of the following:

- The investor could pass on your company because it is in a market that they don't invest in.

- The investor could pass on your company because they already have an investment in a competing technology space.

- The investor could pass because they don't do first-round investments.

- The investor could pass because their fund only covers up to $1 million.

- The investor could offer to create a syndicate to come up with the entire $2 million.

- The investor could identify the specialists needed for an investigation and could set up a follow-up meeting that includes the correct market specialists.

The list goes on and on about possible actions the investor could take. The point is that within a very short time you have set the groundwork for further discussions. On the first contact, the investor will almost never ask for more details. The investor will save the details for the next meeting. And if the investor does ask for more details, the outline of the conversation has already been defined by you in your 15-second speech. You can offer to drill down deeper and in the process maintain a clean, clear flow of information to optimize the discussion with the investor. And the nice thing about the 15-second pitch is that it gives you plenty of room to adjust depending on how the potential investor responds. If the investor says they don't do first rounds, ask whether they can recommend a first-round investor for you to meet with. Every salesperson will tell you, never leave a meeting without gaining something such as a follow-up meeting, a referral, a recommendation, or just an offer to have a drink sometime.

Believe me, I love cool new technology. I love talking about it, reading about it, learning about it, and explaining it. But, I never do it with an investor on the first contact unless they ask for the coolness. I save it for later discussions. Then it will be a well-placed passion with a firm foundation in my 15-second speech.

BOB SHOULD CONSIDER

- Do we have the right executive on board who can present our company "like a banker" would expect?
- Are we trying to sell our "cool" invention to investors rather than trying to explain how they can make money?
- What is our 15-second financial speech?
- Have we practiced how we will respond to every reply the potential investor gives us? Even if we are not salespeople, we need to manage the meeting like we are salespeople and walk away with something valuable.
- How can we utilize a board of advisors to shift us from selling "cool" to potential investors into selling the potential for making money?

Presentation of Valuation

In Chapter 14, "Valuing Innovations," we talked about how to value an invention or innovation. Once you have accumulated the information needed to balance the three time periods, determined how to protect your invention, determined how to make your innovation endure against competition, and maximized the value of your relationships and partners, you must compress all that information into a 60-second speech.

Yes, I am still hung up on timing. I consult with a lot of start-ups. Many of them have spent the bulk of the last six months of their lives producing a 100-page business plan that they expect everyone to be anxious to read. Unfortunately, I don't have time to read all the 100-page business plans that come across my desk. I must be able to determine whether there is a real potential for that start-up in less than a minute or two. Otherwise, I will most likely never return to it.

Don't get me wrong—you will eventually need that business plan. But, it is a long way down the potential investor's road of activities. You have to first make it through one stage at a time before the business plan is anything more than a paperweight. We will discuss the investor meeting process shortly. I have driven start-ups completely through funding without ever producing a 100-page business plan.

BOB SHOULD CONSIDER

- Are we losing our time to market advantage by focusing on producing a business plan when we really need to focus on understanding how to value our invention/innovation?
- If we don't send a potential investor a business plan, what do we send them? The executive summary?
- How can we translate the 60-second speech into a clean sales pitch on paper?

One-Pager

After you have compressed all the wonderful valuation information you have gathered in Chapter 14 and the elevator speeches from the first part of this chapter, you will have a clear and concise summary that covers categories such as these:

- Investment stage, such as seed, first round, second round, and so on
- Investment amount

- Partners, relationships, advisors, and key staff
- Product road map
- Intellectual property
- Invention/innovation
- Market segment
- Market differentiators
- Competitors
- Risks and opportunities

In the start-up investment world, *all* of this information has to be compressed to a single page, called a **one-pager**. It really isn't as hard as it sounds. If you can talk about it all in the 60-second speech, then you may actually find it hard to fill up one page.

If you can't summarize it in a clear, concise manner, then the probability of you ever getting funding is extremely small. Look at it this way: When you browse through books to find one on a topic you are interested in, you probably look at three things: the back cover, the jacket overleaf, and the table of contents. Hmmm . . . the entire book is selling itself to you in the equivalent of what constitutes basically one page.

I prefer a one-pager that is bulleted rather than free-form. I think it is easier to absorb quickly. In addition, if you are having trouble fitting it all on one page, then shifting from free-form to bullets often solves the space issue.

Don't forget that you will need to allocate space on the one-pager for how the investor should contact you for following up. The one-pager must stand alone. Visualize walking around a neighborhood putting a flyer on hundreds of doors. The flyer has to include absolutely everything you want to say to convince the potential customer to call you.

Bob Should Consider

- What should our one-pager look like?
- Do we reveal any "secret sauce" in the one-pager?
- If we can't fit everything on a one pager, what do we leave off?
- How can we test a one-pager before sending it to a potential investor?

Meeting with Investors

I have met with many investors about one start-up company or another. In *all* cases, the sequence of communications between the start-up and the potential investor flowed something like this:

1. Either I made direct contact or a member of my network made direct contact with the VC or angel. The initial contact included forwarding the one-pager for the start-up.

2. Investors who were not interested immediately declined to get involved. In many cases, this was because of a conflict with an investment they already had in place. But there are other reasons that can be negotiated away such as needing a stronger management team.

3. There was a phone call to discuss product, market, competitors, funding, and other topics to validate the VC's understanding of the one-pager and to set up a time for a face-to-face meeting.

4. There was a face-to-face meeting to expand details with multiple representatives of the VC. In *every* case, the VCs showed up with a marked-up version of the one-pager. It was the foundation for our continued discussions.

5. There were follow-up calls and e-mails to establish understanding and interest.

6. The VC began due diligence.

7. The business plan, term sheet, investor deck, and so on, are now needed.

Notice where the one-pager and other information I described earlier are? *Step 1!* Notice where the business plan is? *Step 7!* In between steps 1 and 7, the investor expects you to be able to prove to them that they should remain involved. Otherwise, they don't have the time. And they almost never want to see a business plan until late in the funding process.

BOB SHOULD CONSIDER

- How should we manage investors who are interested but are not willing to move ahead without other investors?

- As we work with potential investors and respond to follow-up questions, should we adjust the one-pager?
- Since the process of working with potential investors can take three to six months, can't we wait to prepare the business plan until after we have started getting initial meetings with investors?

Stealth Disruption

As we discussed in Chapter 14, you will often have to decide between bringing the absolute best product to market and getting a less-capable product to market within a time frame that minimizes risks. In reality, bringing a less-powerful or less-feature-rich product to market can often work to your advantage.

One of the problems with creating a disruptive innovation is that you can kick the innovation life cycles of all your competitors into high gear so that they can follow your disruption. Unless you are the dominant competitor or clearly control intellectual property that protects you, your innovation can quickly be overtaken by more powerful and richer competitors.

By coming to market with less bang, you can avoid creating a market stampede while giving your own product time to evolve into the dominant product even as it garners more and more market share. Although the excitement and fanfare of delivering a product as disruptive as the Apple iPhone or the Nintendo Wii is wonderful, the probability of controlling such a disruption is extremely small.

I am always hesitant to risk it all on a single, highly disruptive innovation. I prefer to enter the market quicker with less fanfare, gauge consumer reaction, adjust the product as needed to drive up transformative value, and then deliver incremental innovations that create a stealth disruption. At some point everyone will realize that the old market is dead, a disruption has occurred, and the consumer's transformative value has completely shifted to a new product. By then, my innovation will be dominant in the new market, and the competitive risks we have discussed throughout this book have been largely avoided.

BOB SHOULD CONSIDER

- Can we take our product to market sooner and safer by following a policy of stealth disruption?

continues

- Should we examine the activities of our competitors to see whether they are following a policy of stealth disruption?

- What functionality or features would we leave out of our product and still come to market with a competitive product?

PART V
Seeing It Work

16

Innovation Use Cases

No matter how exhaustively you analyze historical data, the possibility still exists that your conclusions are based on inaccurate or incomplete assumptions. Applying your plan and conclusions to the real world is the only way to determine the actual risk and reward.

Use Cases, Not Case Studies

Virtually all books on innovation focus on studying the past. They do this by performing a thorough review of different companies and products and then by correlating the results into trends and summations.

Although there have been references to some companies within this book, there has been no usage of case studies. This book by its very title, *Innovate the Future*, is directed at creating innovation, not at focusing on past innovation failures.

These use cases will demonstrate how the material in the book can be used and applied to a diversity of market and products.

The use cases will examine the following topic areas:

- "Use Case 1: Identifying Your Customer"

- "Use Case 2: Targeting Transformative Value"

- "Use Case 3: Limitations on Transformative Value"

- "Use Case 4: Maximizing Lifestyle Integration"

Use Case 1: Identifying Your Customer

It would seem obvious that companies would know who their customers are. But, surprisingly, this is not always the case. Most companies do not consider channel partners, distributors, or even investors as customers. Yet, each of these has a transformative value for a company's product, and each of these transformative values must be maximized in order to maximize the potential of companies and their products.

This use case will describe how utilizing the transformative value chain can assist you in identifying your customers and creating mechanisms to maximize the transformative value of the product to each of the participants in that transformative value chain.

Pharmaceutical Industry Products

When you think about who the customer of a particular drug is, you probably immediately think of the patient. Therefore, you would immediately try to maximize the value of the drug to that consumer and to create marketing materials that specifically target that consumer.

Depending on the cost of the drug and the ways in which the drug is delivered to the patient (pill, liquid, IV, implant, pump, and so on), there can be many participants in the drug's transformative value chain. A low-cost, over-the-counter, commoditized drug like acetaminophen probably has the fewest customers between manufacturing and consumption. Even in these cases, however, the manufacturer has to "sell" the drug to distributors and buyers from the retail outlets and drug stores. These "customers" will maximize the transformative value of even a commoditized drug by buying from the manufacturer that is the lowest priced, most reliable, and easiest to work with.

Expensive Drugs with Complex Delivery Systems

When we look at more expensive drugs with complicated delivery systems, such as implants or external pumps, the transformative value chain expands greatly. Consider the case of a drug, manufactured by the fictional company Z-Drugs, that we will call Miracle. It costs more than $50,000 per year and requires an external pump to deliver the drug in metered doses to targeted areas within the body through an implanted delivery tube. The drug, once delivered, is extremely effective at relieving the patient's symptoms. But, as we shall see, even if we eliminate the distributors, wholesalers, and retail outlets as customers, the transformative value chain for Miracle has at least seven customers within the chain.

There are many roadblocks to delivering a drug like Miracle to the market. Although the benefactors of the drug, the patients, are readily identifiable, the path to actually helping the patient with the drug is extremely complex. Some of the roadblocks on this delivery path include the following:

- **Decision making:** Who makes the decision to proceed with installing a pump through a potentially dangerous surgery?

- **Care giving:** What is the lifestyle impact of the treatment on the caregivers?

- **Delivering:** Who will prescribe and install the delivery system? Who will provide the drug packets used within the delivery pumps?

- **Cost:** Who will bear the cost of the surgery and drug?

- **Risks:** Who will certify the drug as effective, the delivery mechanism as safe, and the procedures as risk-free as possible?

When we examine these questions relative to the drug Miracle, we can quickly see that there are at least seven customers, each of which has a unique transformative value:

- **Patient:** The patient's transformative value is their quality of life.

- **Caregiver:** The caregiver's transformative value is both the quality of life for the loved one (patient) and the potential for simplifying the caregiver's workload by delivering a partial or full cure to the patient.

- **Pharmacist:** The pharmacist's transformative value is related to the complexity of packaging and delivering the drug to the patient/caregiver. The more complex this task becomes, the more likely the pharmacist is going to avoid selling the drug, especially if complexity leads to increased risk.

- **Physician:** The physician's transformative value is driven by income from the surgical procedure and ongoing care for the patient.

- **Device manufacturer:** The pump manufacturer's transformative value is driven by the volume of sales created by the drug delivery system.

- **Payer:** The payer's (insurer or government body) transformative value is driven by a balancing act with perceived value to the patient and cost of alternative, albeit potentially less effective, treatments.

- **Certifier:** The certifier's (such as the U.S. Food and Drug Administration) transformative value is driven by a balancing act of risk/cost of not deploying the treatment against the risk/cost of deploying the treatment.

Simplifying the Product Delivery Chain

It is common for a pharmaceutical company like Z-Drugs to purchase external pumps from a third-party manufacturer. These pump manufacturers will implement any requested software changes in a new version of the pump for the specific drug delivery system defined by Z-Drugs. This relationship can place the pump manufacturer in control of the Z-Drugs product delivery chain, especially if the volume of pumps purchased by Z-Drugs is a relatively small percentage of the pump manufacturer's annual sales.

Most external pumps have a communication port on them that allows the pump to be connected to a computer. Pumps also may have diagnostic software that can be used to query the patient on how their symptoms are responding before administering the next dose of the drug.

Once the pump is connected to a computer, the information can be pulled from the pump. This information can include how many doses of the drug the patient has received, how the patient has rated their "quality" of symptom relief, and any other diagnostics that Z-Drugs has requested be included by the pump manufacturer.

To eliminate the product delivery chain impacts from the pump manufacturer, Z-Drugs can add another partner to the product delivery chain. By building a small device that can be attached externally to the pump, the software components of the Miracle drug delivery system can become independent of the pump. Since this external device is dedicated to the Miracle drug delivery system, this new partner should have a high transformative value to deliver the software requirements quicker than the pump manufacturer. This additional device, let's call it the Linker, is also the foundation for increasing the value of Miracle to all the participants in the transformative value chain.

Maximizing Transformative Value Throughout the Transformative Value Chain

As we discussed earlier, there are at least seven potential "customers" in the delivery path of the Miracle drug. The Z-Drugs company needs to develop the product to maximize the transformative value of Miracle to all of these "customers." One method of doing this is by maximizing the power of the Linker device we attach to the pump to simplify the product delivery chain.

The Linker provides the connection of information and control between the pump and the seven "customers." This information can be used in many ways to maximize individual transformative values:

- **Patient:** The Linker defines how often the patient receives Miracle and also how often the patient can request additional doses. The transformative value of the patient translates directly into quality of life.

- **Caregiver:** The information provided by Linker can be automatically distributed to the caregiver each time the Linker is attached to the patient's computer. This information will provide the caregiver with an understanding of the patient's true quality of life impact from Miracle and will increase the caregiver's comfort level concerning their loved one's overall well being.

- **Pharmacist:** Utilizing information from the Linker, the pharmacist can determine how the drug is being used and how effective it seems. The pharmacist, who is tracking all drugs taken by the patient, can determine whether there are potential side effects occurring based on patient responses to questions asked by the Linker of the patient. The pharmacist can also determine whether the drug package is being used wrong, the pump is not performing correctly, and a wide range of other diagnostic features that could be included with the Linker. These will simplify the pharmacist's tasks and reduce risks. Services by the pharmacist can also increase the pharmacist's revenues.

- **Physician:** The physician, while wanting the best for the patient, actually stands to lose revenues if Miracle is successful. The patient will no longer require as much in-office attention once Miracle starts to work. The Linker data allows the physician to remain an integrated, dynamic decision maker within the Miracle delivery system. The physician can utilize the information from the Linker to perform monthly consultations/reviews of the patient's condition without requiring office time. The doctor can then respond by adjusting the dosage levels with the pharmacist and/or requesting the patient to come into the office for a more detailed follow-up. These ongoing consultations create a continuous revenue stream for the physician.

- **Device manufacturer:** The implementation of the Linker device will provide feedback to the Linker manufacturer on potential new features that could be added to improve the patient's experience as well as the other members of the transformative value chain. These improvements increase the ongoing revenues of the Linker manufacturer.

- **Payer:** Z-Drugs can use the information from all the deployed Linkers to show the payer the cost differential between treatment with Miracle and treatment without. Assuming that Miracle reduces other expenses related to drugs and quality-of-life issues, the payer can see reduced costs with simpler justification.

- **Certifier:** Z-Drugs can use the information derived from the Linker to simplify new submittals to the certifying bodies and accelerate the time to market of new innovations. The certifier can better recognize the improvements in the quality of life of the patients and the real value of the Miracle drug system versus other drug and treatment options.

Benefits to Z-Drugs

Implementing a change in the product delivery chain by including a manufacturing partner to create the Linker has allowed Z-Drugs to benefit in many ways. These go far beyond simplifying the relationship with the external pump manufacturer and include the following:

- **Control of costs:** Creating the Linker commoditizes the pump and allows Z-Drugs to buy pumps off the shelf.

- **Control of features:** The Linker places Z-Drugs in complete control of all features deployed with the drug delivery system Miracle.

- **Time to market:** Z-Drugs, through the Linker, has eliminated external partners in the product delivery chain that could negatively impact time to market. If the current Linker manufacturer does not deliver on time, Z-Drugs has the option of shifting manufacturing, in whole or in part, to other partners.

- **Defensible intellectual property:** The Linker itself is a potentially patentable device. In addition, many of the features within the Linker, the integration portals for each of the customers, and the processes developed to deliver Linker data to the various customers may all be patentable.

Use Case 1 Innovation Take-Aways

In this use case, we applied the following key concepts from the book:

- Review the product delivery chain for ways to simplify.

- Isolate *all* of the customers in the transformative value chain.

- Determine what the factors are that can impact the transformative value of each customer in the transformative value chain.

- Innovate new ways to increase the transformative value for each customer within the transformative value chain.

Use Case 2: Targeting Transformative Value

Throughout this book I have emphasized the critical nature of three factors when it comes to delivering a truly innovative product:

- Target a specific consumer.

- Maximize the lifestyle impact of your product.

- Understand and maximize the transformative value of your product.

No company I have looked at has taken these factors more seriously than LiveComplete. In fact, as we shall see, LiveComplete (www.livecomplete.com) has maximized the usage of these factors almost to perfection.

What Is LiveComplete?

There is a great deal of activity right now in the social networking world. And the biggest activity revolves around how you make money off of the network. The problem is that the concept of making revenue off ad placement has become tiring to many participants within social networks. Once the ads start appearing, many members move to an alternative social network, and the traffic on the social network declines.

LiveComplete has taken a different approach. LiveComplete is an intelligent marketplace and meeting place for living a healthy lifestyle. It has created a customization engine and a social media platform that is targeted at healthy lifestyle-conscious consumers. This can include virtually any consumer, from the soccer mom to the triathlete, who has a desire to improve or maintain their health and wellness. We all know how challenging exercising and eating right can be. Finding like-minded individuals who can boost your moral, offer guidance and advice, or even participate with us can go a long way toward helping us succeed at our health and wellness goals.

But offering just a social media platform dedicated to the health-conscious would not solve the revenue problem. As we will see, LiveComplete has addressed that problem.

Targeting Consumers

Social networks like Facebook or Twitter are normally directed at the masses. All consumers can participate, and any revenue targeting is based mostly on what the consumers read or say in their social interactions. For instance, if someone posted a comment about how they love Stephen King's latest book, suddenly they might start seeing ads related to Stephen King. They would also start getting targeted at other social network members who mention Stephen King. This is an extremely superficial way of targeting consumers. But, this is all that most social networking sites have to go on.

LiveComplete has taken it much, much deeper. Consumers have demonstrated that they are willing to spend regularly on products and services that help them reach their health and wellness goals. The problem arises when the consumer tries to locate a product to meet a specific need or even to identify the need. For instance, if I am a runner, how do I limit thigh cramps? If I am after endurance, what supplements will help me maintain my energy levels? As a novice runner, how would I even know that there are effective ways, through services and products, to maximize my running experience?

Rather than taking a superficial approach to understanding the consumer, LiveComplete allows the consumer to define who they are from a health and wellness perspective. For instance, I can define that I am a runner and a business executive. I can define any number of lifestyles that I lead.

LiveComplete then goes deeper through a patent-pending algorithm and determines how my lifestyle activities are impacting my overall health and wellness. Based on my lifestyle and activity selections, LiveComplete will offer me relevant product, service, and content selections that correlate to my everyday wellness needs and preferences.

LiveComplete understands each individual consumer's needs and how to target products through the following:

- Consumer selection of their wellness, lifestyle, and fitness needs and preferences

- Analyzing consumer needs based on detailed input from subject matter experts

- Targeting relevant products, services, and expert content to those needs and issues

So, how different is LiveComplete's consumer targeting approach? Let's look at the differences in how consumers find specific products and how products are marketed to those consumers:

- **Consumer hunts for a product with a poor understanding of the need:** In this case, the consumer is often unsure of what they need or want, and they have a very hard time completing the purchase. Skincare products are a great example. If I want to buy the right product, I often have to know whether I have oily, regular, or dry skin. Frankly, I have no idea what kind of skin I have.

- **Superficial targeting:** In this case, the consumer may have no need at all, and the ad is a complete nuisance. Worse, the consumer may click the ad, costing the advertiser revenue dollars even though the consumer never completes a purchase. Potentially thousands of impressions of the same ad get displayed to garnish a few clicks. And of these clicks, only a very small percent will turn into a sale for the advertiser.

- **Consumer understands their issue but not the product needed:** I experienced this recently. The door on our dishwasher fell open and slammed into the floor. Obviously, a spring or something had broken. I went to a parts-supply website and drilled down into the parts list of my dishwasher and eventually ordered a spring. I was unsure if I had purchased the right spring or even if I had determined the right problem/need until the spring showed up a week later.

- **Consumer is shown their potential need and shown meaningful products, services, content, and connectivity:** By understanding the consumer's activities, demographics, and other key information, products can be targeted optimally to the consumer.

BOB SHOULD CONSIDER

- What can we do to maximize our ability to target the consumer?
- Are we taking a "superficial approach" to targeting consumers?
- Can we orient our product offerings on a consumer-by-consumer basis?

Maximizing Lifestyle Impact

When I go on a business trip, there is little I can do to actively fix my dishwasher. But, when it comes to my health and wellness activities, this is not true. I can still run, exercise in the hotel gym, or even get together with someone locally for a game of racquetball. But, without LiveComplete's customized recommendations and social networking capabilities, I would have to already know someone local to my business trip destination.

LiveComplete lets me sync up with people with similar lifestyles and activities to me. The potential for impacting my lifestyle skyrockets. I can plan to get together with a LiveComplete networking buddy for an hour of swimming at the hotel. Not only will I make a new friend, but we will both be doing what we enjoy.

Additionally, let's assume that I am in a triathlete training program when I suddenly need to travel for three weeks. Unfortunately, my coach can't come with me. LiveComplete will help me identify coaches who specialize in my type of training throughout my travels. I don't have to put my healthy lifestyle on hold while taking care of my business lifestyle requirements.

The staying power of any brand and the up-sell capabilities are based largely on the **stickiness** of the brand's product. This stickiness is a factor of how deeply the product penetrates our lifestyles. The deeper the penetration, the greater the stickiness. LiveComplete separates the stickiness from the actual product. And then LiveComplete recombines them.

How does LiveComplete accomplish this remarkable separation and yet connection at the same time? It does so by understanding the lifestyles, activities, and needs of the consumer and applying that knowledge independently to both social networking and relevant offerings. But, LiveComplete then combines the powers of social networking with product selection. Let's break it down:

- LiveComplete understands my needs and issues based on lifestyles and activities.

- LiveComplete allows me to create in minutes a social network with people with similar lifestyles and activities. Highly targeted networking: very sticky!

- My LiveComplete social network actively supports my health and wellness activities. Direct integration into my lifestyles: very sticky!

- LiveComplete offers me products, services, and content that are targeted directly based on my needs and issues. Highly targeted offerings for me: very sticky!

- If I have a question about a particular product or a wellness issue, I can see on the LiveComplete website other people who have the same issues and needs and who have purchased this specific product. I can directly ask these fellow social networkers their opinions. If they are online, I could even do it in real time. This creates the potential for a very high sales completion rate and increased customer satisfaction: very sticky!

BOB SHOULD CONSIDER

- How can we expand the lifestyle penetration of our products?
- How sticky are our products?
- How can we increase the stickiness of our products?

Maximize Transformative Value

As we have seen in the innovation life cycle, it becomes increasingly difficult to maintain a positive transformative value for a product. Eventually, the product enters the negative areas of the life cycle, and through negative and destructive inventions, the transformative value begins to fall and leads to eventual product commoditization.

LiveComplete has taken a unique approach by maximizing lifestyle integration and dynamically adjusting its targeted offering to maximize the transformative value on a per-consumer basis. For instance, if I decide to change my running activities in some way, LiveComplete will automatically adjust my recommendations to maximize my success in my modified activities.

Throughout this book, I have tried to emphasize the need to constantly monitor the lifestyles of your consumers and the transformative value of your product so that you can detect any changes that may be occurring because of new market innovations. LiveComplete has implemented their smart technology so that it adapts to the health and wellness lifestyles of their consumers. This allows LiveComplete to completely adjust its offerings in real time so that the transformative value of the offerings is always maximized. I can not currently visualize a competitive model that can displace a properly deployed LiveComplete offering.

> ### BOB SHOULD CONSIDER
>
> - Are we effectively monitoring the changes in our consumer's lifestyles? Can we adjust our understanding in real time?
>
> - Is there a way for us to dynamically adjust the transformative value of our product offerings?

Use Case 2 Innovation Take-Aways

In this use case, we applied the following key concepts from the book:

- Maintain a foundational "good enough" product that can be modified to attack separate niche markets.

- Develop a product offering that maximizes the transformative value for each individual consumer group.

- Monitor each consumer group to detect shifts within the group, and adjust the product offering to maintain transformative value.

- Drive products into the consumer's lifestyle to maintain maximum stickiness and to ward off competition.

Use Case 3: Limitations on Transformative Value

I thought that one use case should focus on a product group/industry that has a virtually impossible mission when it comes to new product innovation. One such industry is the soft drink industry, which includes all clear and dark sodas and colas.

From the perspective of product innovation, here are the key factors that I find interesting about the soft drink industry:

- The products are very simple, consisting of basically water and a few ingredients.

- Product innovation is almost impossible.

- The brand name is a major part of a product's transformative value and limits almost all innovation opportunities.

- Convenience drives brand loyalty.

Product Innovation

Producing a bottle of soda appears to be far simpler than producing a glass of milk. There are no animals to feed and care for, no complicated collection systems, no purification processes like homogenization, and very few issues with shelf life or refrigeration. Sodas can be produced from mostly local supplies (water) in a single building, reducing the shipping costs and supply chain issues. Excess inventory can be retained for long periods and delivered to meet future sales demand. So, why does a gallon of name-brand soda cost as much or more than a gallon of milk?

Part of the distinction between sodas and milk is that milk is a commodity in the most absolute sense. When you think of drinking milk, you seldom think about what dairy or type of cow the milk came from. Soda, although a commodity, is highly linked to a particular manufacturer.

By virtually any measure, the soft drink industry is highly commoditized:

- The products of all major brand competitors consistently sell at more or less the same price, except when one is placed on sale.

- Lesser-known brands, or private-label brands, consistently sell successfully for much less than name brands.

- The addition of new features does not justify an increase in cost and often damages the market share.

There have been multiple "cola wars" over the past several decades where companies attempted to increase their soft drink market share. Surprisingly, these wars had virtually nothing to do with enhancing the product. They were marketing wars designed to shift a consumer's brand loyalty through enhanced product perception. But, many soft drink consumers don't care whether a majority of tasters preferred an alternative brand. These consumers are extremely loyal to their chosen brand/taste. And since the prices are always the same, why bother changing?

Many soft drink manufacturers have tried to innovate new enhancements of their products. But, consumers segregate soft drinks based on only a few criteria:

- Color, such as dark or clear

- Flavor, such as cola, lemon-lime, cherry, and so on

- Sugar or diet

- Caffeine or no caffeine

What is truly amazing about the consumer is that the consumer is rarely willing to accept a major change in any of these categories when the resulting product still has the same manufacturer's name. A dark-cola manufacturer will likely have little success creating a clear soda with the same name, even if the taste is exactly the same. Consumers have likely already selected a clear soda and have no incentive to change.

If the product itself doesn't allow innovation, what is left? There are primarily three transformative value factors that will affect a consumer's willingness to change soft drinks:

- Cost

- Brand loyalty

- Convenience

In some cases, brand loyalty will override all other considerations and completely eliminate any shifts outside of a particular name brand manufacturer. If the preferred brand of dark cola is not conveniently available, then the consumer will shift to a clear soda by the same manufacturer. When asked why, the consumer will respond with, "I don't like XYZ's sodas."

Cost, as we discussed, is almost never a factor since all name-brand sodas are priced the same. In fact, in all situations of nonbulk sales, the price is always the same for a bottle or a cup of soda regardless of whether it is a name-brand soda and regardless of the type (dark/clear, sugar/no sugar, and caffeine/no caffeine).

BOB SHOULD CONSIDER

- Does our product fall into a market with similar restrictions to the soft drink market?

- If we are unable to directly deliver new innovations to the product itself, what other ways can we use to increase the transformative value of our product?

- In a situation like the soft drink market, would a company be better served by focusing all innovation efforts on increasing the convenience factor and ignore attempts to change/expand the existing product line?

- What other commoditized markets could the "convenience" factor be applied to?

Convenience Drives Brand Loyalty

Convenience therefore is the one remaining factor that will have a huge impact on customer brand loyalty. The soda brand carried by each major fast-food company is the number-one and most critical factor in a soda manufacturer's ability to innovate and drive new sales. I am not much of a soda drinker, so I choose fast food based on the food quality and taste. I have friends who choose the fast-food chain based on their ability to get their preferred brand of soda.

Surprisingly, the breadth of convenience also appears to drive bulk purchases of sodas in supermarkets. Consumers could save significantly on their soda budget by buying store brands of sodas. Yet, most people I have talked to are unwilling to try, let alone drink regularly, anything other than their regular brand. Once again, cost is not a major factor. Since most off-brand sodas are not available in fast-food restaurants, it is very difficult for the brands to penetrate and compete regardless of their quality and taste.

Convenience therefore appears to be the one lifestyle impact that drives over time virtually all consumers' soda selections. When the only factor that can impact transformative value is one that has little or nothing to do with product innovation, we can quickly see why new product offerings fail. There is limited space for new soda types in fast-food restaurants regardless of the manufacturer. Although many consumers may love a vanilla-flavored dark soda, the inability to get one on a regular basis will dramatically impact purchasing decisions and limit market penetration. In fact, the probability of any new soda manufacturer garnering more than a small share of the market is amazingly small unless one can overcome the convenience factor.

So, if we are loyal to our regular soda manufacturer, why do the large manufacturers run all the ad campaigns? It is to back up the fast-food chain's decision to pick a particular brand of sodas for the chain's restaurants. Innovative advertising creates new convenience possibilities that have the potential over time to shift brand loyalty.

BOB SHOULD CONSIDER

- In the case of the soft drink market, convenience appears to be a factor with a circular impact on consumer buying. Are there other factors that have a similar impact on consumer buying and the venue of the purchase?

continues

- How can a new market entrant gain market penetration, that is, convenience, in a situation like the soft drink market?
- If convenience has such a huge impact on bulk and follow-up sales, would it be reasonable to offer drastically reduced prices to fast-food chains in order to get market visibility and increase the convenience impact?

Use Case 3 Innovation Take-Aways

In this use case, we applied the following key concepts from the book:

- Attempting to increase the transformative value of a highly commoditized product is extremely difficult if not impossible.

- The transformative value of a commoditized product is still defined primarily by lifestyle impact. Adjusting this lifestyle impact, rather than adding new features, is often the only way to shift transformative value between competitors.

- Companies should utilize their intellectual property (supply chain, manufacturing, and distribution) to penetrate alternative markets with similar products.

Use Case 4: Maximizing Lifestyle Integration

Lifestyle integration: If you want to control how a consumer spends their limited resources, then you need to control their purchases by becoming deeply integrated into their lifestyle.

I'm not much of a mall shopper. If I need something, I go to a particular store, make my purchase, and leave. I think part of it is that I really don't have a lot of spare time to stroll the mall looking around. Part of it is also that I don't generally buy things on the spur of the moment. I have a need, and I purchase something to fill it. But, with a large active family, it is not always easy to remember what I actually need (OK, age has something to do with it as well). It would be nice if the mall would actually remind me of what I need.

So, what would make me start shopping more at the mall? It would have to be something that allows an integration of the stores and their products with my lifestyle—something that guided me to the things that I might be interested in purchasing in addition to the things I need, rather than requiring that I stumble around for hours hoping to bump into something I might like. It would be nice if the mall told me where to shop and if the mall gave me the best prices.

Sometimes I buy one thing and discover that I really need three more things in order to use what I just bought. Maybe I bought a framed painting in an import store. Now I need nails and framing wire. Where do I get those? Or I just bought my kids a new game console on sale. Now I want to get some games for it on sale as well, but the store I am in doesn't sell a variety of games, or their prices are too high. Where do I get the games? It would be nice if the mall knew what I was buying and guided me to my additional purchases.

Does that sound like I am visualizing an omniscient mall? Well, not really omniscient. But, I am visualizing a mall that maximizes the shopping experience and the number of purchases for each consumer. This sounds to me what a mall should be for. Let's call it the Smart Mall.

BOB SHOULD CONSIDER

- Does our product, like the shopping mall, fall into a category of love it or hate it?
- How applicable is the Smart Mall concept to an online shopping experience?
- Wouldn't the shopping experience of a megastore like Wal-Mart also be enhanced by a Smart Mall approach?

Technology for the Smart Mall

The technology is available right now to implement the Smart Mall. Here is what is needed:

- Smartphones or a mall-supplied shopping device
- Mall integration with point-of-sale systems in the stores
- Location-awareness hardware and software
- LCD screens as point-of-sale displays

How each of these components plays a part will become clear through the discussion of the Smart Mall. Here is how the Smart Mall would work:

1. The consumer registers their smartphone upon entering the mall. Consumers will have an account that allows them to accumulate shopping credits and apply these to all stores in the mall for discounts or other specials.

2. If the consumer does not have a smartphone, the mall will provide a simple presentation device that cannot be removed from the mall. Again, this device will be integrated into a consumer mall account.

3. Shoppers can select categories of items they are interested in, such as women's shoes or imported chocolates. There would be no requirement to make such a selection unless the consumer has a specific need.

4. The shopper is directed to specific stores with on-screen product pictures, prices, and directions.

5. As the shopper moves around within the mall, the smartphone or mall device communicates with location sensors so that software knows where the consumer is within the mall and whether they are moving.

6. If a consumer stops moving, the location software correlates that with products in the area. The consumer may be examining particular products, and these will be added to the consumer's potential shopping list.

7. The consumer selects and makes a purchase.

8. The point-of-sale system notifies the mall system of the consumer's purchase. The mall system adjusts the consumer's potential shopping list to correlate to the new purchase. If the consumer purchased red women's high heels, perhaps a black evening dress will be shown.

9. If the consumer selects to view the dress and heads toward that store, the mall system begins to adjust the potential shopping list yet again to strengthen the women's clothing preference.

10. The consumer leaves the mall. The Smart Mall remembers the purchases, preferences, and shopping style of the consumer.

Each time the consumer's potential shopping list is changed, the entire mall will start to react differently. As the consumer moves throughout the mall, the mall will analyze which shoppers are nearest to LCD monitors and will decide what products to display that will maximize each shopper's potential of making another purchase. Our example shopper with the women's high heels might start seeing dresses of similar styles or a matching handbag.

For all intents and purposes, the consumer's mall shopping experience is now the product being offered by the mall. With the Smart Mall, the experience itself has a dynamically adjusting transformative value that has the ability to increase the transformative value of all items on the consumer's potential shopping list.

BOB SHOULD CONSIDER

- Are there technology "wrappers" that we could use to enhance the consumer's experience of purchasing our products?

- Will creating an overarching transformative value for all of our products increase the individual transformative value for each of our products?

- How can we increase our product's transformative value by providing the consumer with an easy method of locating and choosing products that integrate with our own?

Transformative Value Chain

In the case of the Smart Mall, there is not just one entity benefiting. There are actually at least four different entities in the transformative value chain:

- **The manufacturers:** The product manufacturers want to maximize sales of their products.

- **The mall:** The mall wants to maximize the amount of money the consumer spends so that the stores will be willing to pay higher fees.

- **The store:** The store wants to maximize sales.

- **The consumer:** The consumer wants to get the best deal available, wants to find their purchases quickly, and wants to benefit from being a loyal Smart Mall shopper.

Remember, as we discussed earlier in the book, the ability to maximize the revenue potential for all players in the transformative value chain is critical to sustaining the transformative value to the consumer.

> ### BOB SHOULD CONSIDER
>
> - Are there entities in our product's transformative value chain that we normally do not consider when we are trying to maximize the consumer's transformative value for our product?
> - By implementing a blended product experience like the shopping experience offered by the Smart Mall, can we create a direct and profitable linkage with other entities in the transformative value chain?

Benefits to the Manufacturers

The manufacturer will get maximum exposure of their products directed at the consumer who is most likely to make a purchase. Walk into virtually any store in a mall, and you will be overwhelmed by the diversity of products and the time needed to make a proper selection. When I walk into an unfamiliar store, I almost immediately walk up to a salesclerk and ask for directions to the item I am looking for. As I said, I don't want to hunt all day for the right matching product. I want to have someone, or something, point me directly to everything I need. The Smart Mall grants my wish while allowing for the implementation of a manufacturer preference within the preferred shopping list based on the advertising budget of the product manufacturer and my spending limits.

If the consumer repeatedly ignores suggestions for high-end purchases and instead selects a less-expensive alternative, then the Smart Mall can adjust accordingly and can even display a pros and cons checklist that compares the two products. Perhaps the consumer would be willing to purchase the high-end product given the right information?

The manufacturer gets real-time marketing that is directly targeted at the correct consumer.

Benefits to the Store

The store gets the potential for sales not only from first-time buyers during their current mall shopping experience but also for follow-up sales from other stores within the mall. By adding their product database to the Smart Mall, the store gets targeted advertising to a potential purchaser who has already made a qualifying purchase in a different store.

Each store could define different criteria of how to respond to an external purchase. If our consumer bought an evening gown, perhaps a jewelry store would be willing to offer a 30% instant discount of matching jewelry. For a lower-priced dress, the jewelry store might offer only a 5% discount.

This model allows the store to adjust in real time the transformative value of each particular product targeted at a specific consumer. Instead of offering a discount to all shoppers at random, the discounts are highly targeted so as to create follow-up sales.

Consider the possibility that the consumer comes to the jewelry store based on the addition of matching jewelry to the potential shopping list. Now the staff in the jewelry store can be notified of the potential preferences of the consumer. In addition, the display ads will shift to display the matching jewelry. So, the store becomes a Smart Store with staff members who are instantly trained to the consumer.

Consider further that the consumer leaves the mall without purchasing jewelry. Two weeks later the consumer returns to the mall and starts shopping for other items. The Smart Mall can inform the consumer that the jewelry is still available, and the discount has been increased just for her.

The store gets the potential to control customer experience, to maximize the capabilities of store personnel, and to drive targeted, real-time advertising at repeat customers.

Consumer discounts could be funded in real time from fees that the mall collects from the manufacturers and the stores to provide a level of sales guarantees for the fees paid without suffering undue costs from discounts.

Benefits to the Mall

The mall makes money from everyone except potentially the consumer. The consumer could also be a revenue source depending on the types of services and products that the mall sells directly such as package wrapping and shipping.

The mall makes money from the manufacturers who pay a fee to have their products displayed on mall-based LCD monitors to prospective shoppers. These fees can also impact the initial product-offering rank similar to a bidding arrangement. If one shoe manufacturer pays a higher fee, then that manufacturer's red high heels would be displayed in preference to a different manufacturer paying a lower fee.

The mall makes money from the stores who pay a fee to participate in the Smart Mall and perhaps pay a commission for each sale directed to the store. The commission could be a sliding scale based on amount of discount offered, total purchase amount, and so on.

All stores in the mall would be compelled to join the Smart Mall because of the potential inclusion of their competitors. The mall could offer a sign-up discount to the first ten stores. Once traffic begins, all other stores would see the benefit and follow along. Any potential negatives to any one store could be counterbalanced by adjustable fees based on traffic and sales results.

An additional benefit to the mall and the stores within the mall is that they become a collective sales front that can compete effectively against large chain megamarts.

Benefits to the Consumer

The consumer gets the overriding benefit of having a shopping experience that is dynamically designed to do the following:

- Maximize the overall shopping experience.

- Minimize the time needed to complete the shopping experience.

- Maximize the odds that the consumer will find the "right" product without exhaustive shopping.

- Minimize the cost of purchases. The consumer will receive the effective benefits of making one large mall purchase rather than many purchases at different stores. The discounts would rise based on the overall shopping experience, not just a single purchase.

- Direct access to the product catalog of the entire mall in real time.

- Give loyalty discounts across the mall.

The benefits to the consumer could go on and on. The simple facts that the consumer is being targeted dynamically with the optimal product mix and that the transformative value can be maximized at all times make this a guaranteed success.

BOB SHOULD CONSIDER

- The Smart Mall has the potential not only to create revenues for the mall's tenants but also to increase revenues to the mall from alternative sources. Does such a relationship potential exist for our products?

- Technologies have changed dramatically over the past several years with the introduction of smartphones, netbooks, and other devices. Have we considered the impact of these devices on our ability to deliver our product and increase our product's transformative value?

- The Smart Mall concept started by looking at the things that impact the transformative value of the mall shopping experience, not the products sold within the mall. Is there a similar, higher-level viewpoint that could benefit our products?

Use Case 4 Innovation Take-Aways

In this use case, we applied the following key concepts from the book:

- Understanding the lifestyles and needs of your consumers is critical to innovating new products and services.

- Focusing on increasing revenues rather than on increasing transformative value can cause you to miss innovation opportunities that are "outside the box" and that drive new revenues.

- Isolating your intellectual property from your products allows you to blend in new inventions and create new innovations.

- Always address the transformative value of all participants in the transformative value chain.

Index

→ Consulting and services firm, churning out innov. products?

→ we have developed outsourcing rel. mgmt sks → currently, it is similar to other prdts in the market.

→ we have to einnovate further to create a difere...
→ what do we do?

→ All prds rt. now focused primarily on client. Vendor needs importance too.

→ Most prds also focused on big picture, not on opr activities that actually form the core g a good client – vendor rel.

→ our next incremental innov should be on proj mgmt, change mgmt, workflow ...

→ we have been developing on the cloud, continu to to so → work out how much it cost, figure out cost-of ct. offering → price it at a few 100s more.

FREE Online Edition

Your purchase of **Innovate the Future** includes access to a free online edition for 45 days through the Safari Books Online subscription service. Nearly every Prentice Hall book is available online through Safari Books Online, along with more than 5,000 other technical books and videos from publishers such as Addison-Wesley Professional, Cisco Press, Exam Cram, IBM Press, O'Reilly, Que, and Sams.

SAFARI BOOKS ONLINE allows you to search for a specific answer, cut and paste code, download chapters, and stay current with emerging technologies.

Activate your FREE Online Edition at
www.informit.com/safarifree

> **STEP 1:** Enter the coupon code: LVUHQVH.

> **STEP 2:** New Safari users, complete the brief registration form. Safari subscribers, just log in.

If you have difficulty registering on Safari or accessing the online edition, please e-mail customer-service@safaribooksonline.com